LONDON'S STATUES OF WOMEN

Juliet Rix is an award-winning writer, editor and broadcaster working for national newspapers, magazines and the BBC. She has a degree in History of Art and Natural Sciences and has written two other non-fiction books for adults and two fiction books for children. She has travelled in more than 60 countries but always returns to her beloved home city – London.

www.julietrix.com   @julietrix1

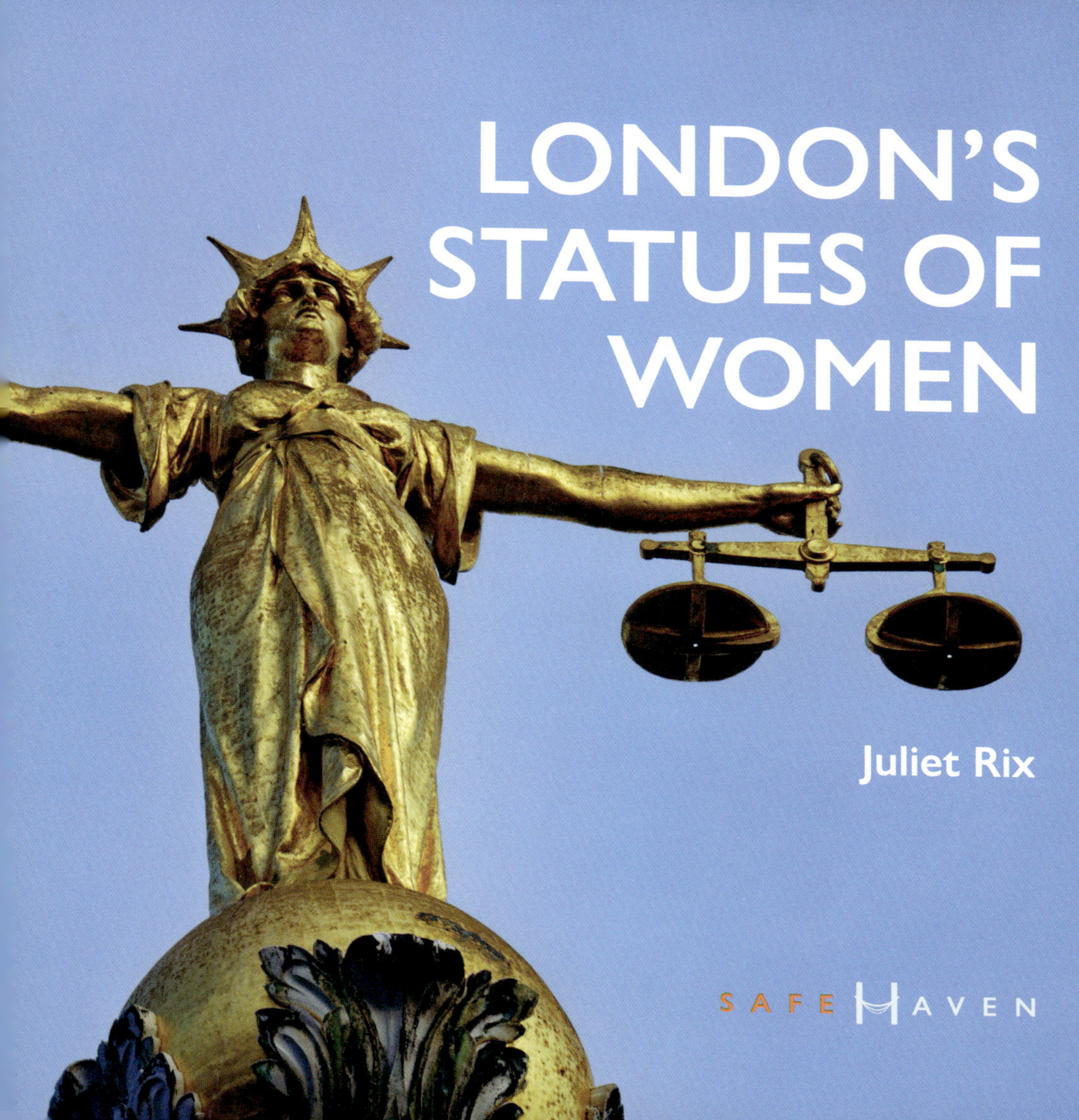

LONDON'S STATUES OF WOMEN

Juliet Rix

SAFE HAVEN

To my husband Rod and sons Daniel and Luke
– and all the wonderful family and friends who
recently got me through a difficult couple of years.

First published 2025 by
Safe Haven Books Ltd
12 Chinnocks Wharf
42 Narrow Street
London E14 8DJ
www.safehavenbooks.co.uk

A catalogue record for this book is available from the British Library.

ISBN 978 1 0685162 0 7
10 9 8 7 6 5 4 3 2 1
2028 2027 2026 2025

Typeset in Trade Gothic and Mrs Eaves XL Serif
designed by TimPetersDesign.co.uk
Printed and bound in the UK by Bell & Bain, Glasgow

The Safe Haven team on *London's Statues of Women*: Juliet Rix,
Rod Standing, Graham Coster, Tim Peters, David Welch, Lesley
MacKay, Catherine Fenton

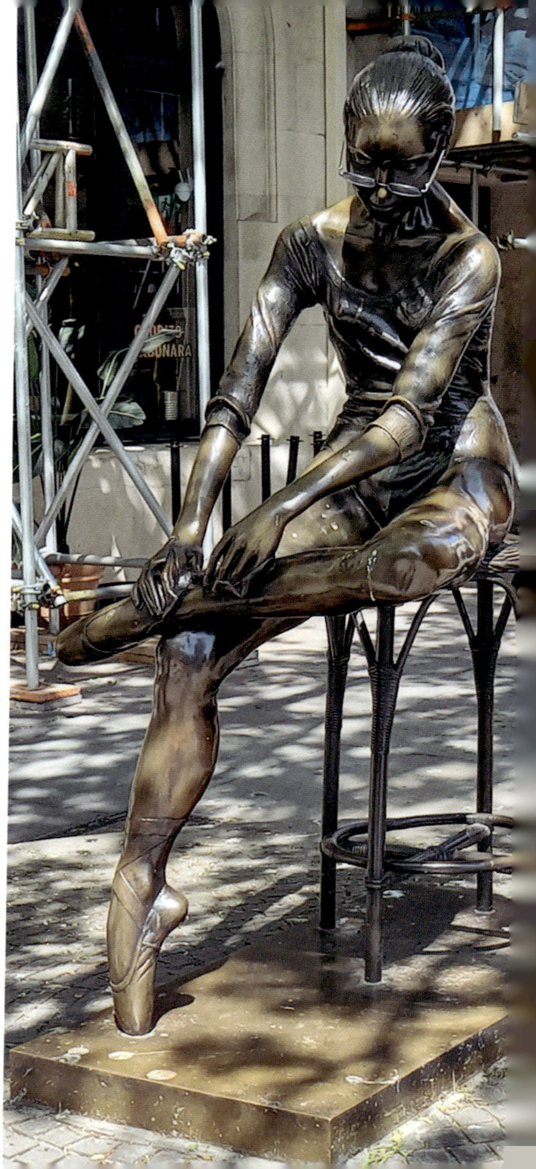

Acknowledgements

Primary thanks go to Graham Coster of Safe Haven Books who initiated this book and gave me the privilege of writing it, before seeing it through to the bookshelves. Thanks too to my husband Rod for his patience and support while I researched, wrote, edited and angsted; for periodically pounding the streets with me from statue to statue; and for many of the photographs, especially those requiring a zoom lens. And to my writer son Luke – one of the best editors I know – who kindly went through much of the manuscript before submission (but not all – any misses are mine!).

I am grateful to individual historians and others n organisations from the Bank of England and English Heritage to St Pancras Station and Somerset House who took the time to answer my questions, to sculptors and relatives of the commemorated who shared their thoughts with me. And of course to the writers and researchers who have walked some of these routes before me, producing websites like Art UK, Bob Speel and Ornamental Passions, and books including *London's Immortals* (John Blackwood, 1989) and Philip Ward-Jackson's impeccably researched Public Sculpture catalogues of the City (2003) and Westminster (2011).

Finally, I am grateful to family and friends who took an encouraging interest in the book and its progress, and particularly to Richard and Claire who pointed out one last statue just in time. I hope all of them will enjoy the resulting book.

A note about this book

This book is designed to be dipped into. It can be read in any order, anywhere, anytime. It can also, if you wish, serve as a field guide on statue safaris around the streets of London. At the back you'll find three Statue Safaris – guided walks around parts of central London particularly clustered with statues. Please keep to the pavement and always cross the road at designated crossing points.

The geographic index is there to help you find groups of statues close together or discover other figures nearby when you are visiting a particular place.

Happy hunting, on pavements or simply in these pages.

Picture credits

All pictures by Juliet Rix except:

Graham Coster: 1, 4, 61 (top), 105, 113, 134 (right), 202

Rod Standing: 2-3, 8, 9, 29, 42, 43, 44, 45 (top and bottom right), 46, 47 (right), 49, 56 (right), 57, 82-3, 90-1, 92-3, 99, 111, 124 (right), 151 (right), 176 (left), 178 (right), 179, 187, 197, 210, 213

Alamy: 10, 16, 18, 22, 24, 28 (left), 30, 35 (top right), 48, 54 (right), 56 (left), 58 (left), 64, 66 (right), 68 (right), 80, 84 (left), 94, 104, 106 (right), 120, 126, 128 (right), 134 (left), 140, 142, 154, 163 (left), 172, 174, 176 (right), 180, 192, 200, 204 (right), 205, 208 (left)

Courtesy of Mary Millner: 12-13

Courtesy of Marc Quinn: 19

James O. Jenkins: 23 (right)

Courtesy of Mark Evans: 26

Bank of England Archive: 42, 81 (ref. 5A13/1/1/61/6)

Salvation Army: 52 (right)

Lucie Skeaping: 74

Kevin Atherton: 88 (right), 89

Dan Burman, londonphotographer.co.uk: 96

Fr Emmanuel: 113

Tim Peters: 130, 190 (right), 191 (left)

Maureen Paley Gallery: 137

Illustrated London News, Mary Evans: 185 (left)

Jessica Wetherly (190 (left)

Neddy Seagoon, Wikicommons: 211

English Heritage: 212

© Crown copyright IWM (CM 5322): 214

Contents

Introduction

'Won't that be a short book?' was often the reply when I said I was writing a book about statues of women in London. Shorter than a book about statues of men, certainly – but also, I would contend, more varied and intriguing.

The men on pedestals are mostly soldiers or statesmen; the females are a fascinating mix. Some extraordinary women's lives are wrapped up in metal and stone on our streets: spies and war nurses, actresses and activists, even a 'poetical mathematician' and the occasional 'ordinary bod'. And of course there are queens – a remarkable group of women thrust to the fore in a man's world.

A 2021 survey found that just one in six of London's statues commemorating a named individual were for women. But 2022 and 2023 saw more statues of women installed than of men, and 2023 alone welcomed five new statues of individual women. Things have fallen back since, but vastly more statues of women have been unveiled in London in the last decade than ever before.

In fact, we are living in a statue boom time – the installation of all kinds of statues is at an all-time high. From the late 1600s to 1820 London saw an average of one new free-standing full-length statue *per decade*, rising to five in the 1830s, -40s and -50s. The Victorian and Edwardian eras brought an Imperial 'statue mania', with multiplying monuments to individual 'heroes' and to Queen Victoria, plus an explosion of newly vivacious 'New Sculpture'

The first statue of a non-royal woman in London: Sarah Siddons in 1987

figures on architectural facades. The First World War shifted attention to war memorials, and only in the late twentieth century did things really pick up again. Since then, numbers have kept rising.

It has been said that you can judge a society by its public statues. You might think they'd reflect only the elite with the power to install them, but most have been erected by public subscription, following a campaign, or by politicians or companies keen to reflect their voters' or customers' values. Though not a perfect reflection, they do hold up a mirror to the preoccupations of the day.

London's first statue of a named non-royal woman squeaked in just before the start of the twentieth century. Many people assume it was

Florence Nightingale – and she is the UK's most commemorated non-royal woman – but this honour went to celebrity actress Sarah Siddons, in 1897.

Over the following 25 years, only four more statues of named non-royal women were unveiled – and this was during the 'golden age' of statuary. The first quarter of this century, however, saw 24 such figures installed – partly a conscious attempt at rebalancing by campaigners, local authorities and the office of the London Mayor. The first statue of a real woman of colour appeared only in 1986.

London, though, has long been peopled with a crowd of classical female figures – decorative, symbolic, mythological, allegorical, anything but real. Virtues such as Courage and Justice 'are seldom depicted [as] men,' observed the architect Sir Hugh Casson. Why? Perhaps partly because when men are seen as the doers, their symbolic helpers – like their mothers, wives, and ships – will inevitably be imagined female. Many are also semi-naked; an astonishing number of bare breasts overlook London's streets, and most date to periods famously prudish about actual women.

This book cannot cover all these symbolic women, nor is there room for graves, low reliefs or anything not visible from an outdoor public space. But alongside plenty of remarkable real women, we will take a look at a few key characters like Justice and Britannia.

Like most Londoners I grew up walking past my city's statues without a sideways – or upward – glance.

... and one of the most recent: the National Windrush Monument, 2022

My first inkling that I was missing something was when I was taken as a teenager to Brussels and was clearly meant to be impressed by the Grand Place. It made me realise how I underappreciated London – and particularly Parliament Square. But it still took campaigner Caroline Criado-Perez, years later, to point out that there was not a single woman memorialised in this iconic location, and to get Millicent Fawcett installed for the centenary of women's suffrage.

Now I'm aware of London's parallel population – stationary but not unmoving – and I'm delighted to introduce you to some of its amazing women.

Juliet Rix
London, 2025

Ada Lovelace Bronze, 2022

By Mary and Etienne Millner

Millbank Quarter, Horseferry Rd, Westminster, SW1 3GE, junction with Dean Bradley St (visible when walking towards the river only)

See also: interview with co-sculptor Mary Millner (p. 12-13)

It's a shame this statue is so high up; it deserves to be noticed. It was commissioned 'to add a female scientific pioneer' to the 1920s statues of male scientists that adorn the neighbouring building – the former HQ of ICI (Imperial Chemical Industries).

Based on a from-life portrait by Margaret Sarah Carpenter that hangs in 10 Downing Street, Ada Lovelace (1815–52) stands here in a Victorian silk gown, a lady of her time. But behind her are two giant golden punch cards (with hidden puzzles for the in-the-know), firmly referencing her contribution to early computing.

Lovelace was born Ada Byron, the only legitimate child of the Romantic poet Lord Byron. Ada never knew her notorious father, who left England weeks after her birth never to return. She was, however, fascinated by him and called her first child Byron, despite – or perhaps because of – her domineering mother's antipathy and unconcealed concern that the daughter might take after the father to become 'mad, bad and dangerous to know'.

Lady Byron was often absent but, an educationalist and tiger mother, she ensured that the sickly Ada studied hard and was well taught, including by Mary Somerville (of the Oxford college). Socially well connected, in 1833 mother and 17-year-old daughter attended a soirée at the home of Charles Babbage, inventor of the digital programmable computer. It was the start of a lifelong connection.

Ada later worked on an article about Babbage's Analytical Engine, which led to her being called 'the first computer programmer'. She wasn't. But she was an accomplished, innovative mathematician admired even by Michael Faraday, and dubbed by Babbage 'an enchantress of numbers'.

Calling her approach 'poetical science', Ada was – crucially – the first to recognise that Babbage's machines could do more than number-crunch. Since numbers could represent other entities that were manipulable according to rules, she reasoned, computers might even make music.

She was no shrinking violet, and did not always allay

Ada Lovelace's discussion of calculus in one of her letters.

her mother's fears.
In her teens she eloped
with a tutor, but was
caught. The affair
was hushed up, and
two years later she
married William King-
Noel, soon 1st Earl of
Lovelace. Rumours
of her extra-marital
affairs swirled – some
probably true – and she
was prone to gamble,
losing substantial
sums, particularly
when her 'winning'
mathematical
formula failed.

She died painfully
of uterine cancer
aged just 36, but
her work prevails,
and now the second
Tuesday in October
is Ada Lovelace Day,
celebrating women's
contribution to STEM
– science, technology,
engineering and
maths.

An Interview with Mary Millner

'Many people passing a statue of a woman in a Victorian dress will think it's just another Queen Victoria [see p. 164], so we wanted to be very clear that she isn't. We needed to portray her work and her links with now – hence the punch cards.

'There are not enough statues of women, and not enough statues to do with science, so we loved this commission. We simplified the Carpenter portrait but stayed close to it. A lot of public art stays close to

well-known images because they resonate – they're recognisable, and that's important.

'I think as artists we've all been thinking recently about whether statues of individuals are appropriate. I think about this a lot. You can run away from the question and put little bronze birds on poles as Tracey Emin has done (she has said it is less oppressive than traditional public art), but I wouldn't want everyone to do that. Maggi Hambling did something bold with

her Mary Wollstonecraft [p. 128], but I like the concept more than the work.

'I think what went on in Bristol probably landed in the right place: the slave-owner went into the river, and then into a museum with a notice attached. That's great – it continues the story.

'I do think there is value in representational public art. We need reminders of the people who were here before us – the layers of history. And I don't think anything does that so well as a full-size statue.

'I stop and look at statues as I walk through London. I love knowing Mozart was in this part of Pimlico, to be reminded of Nelson Mandela, to think about the Windrush arrivals [p. 208], and what happened to Charles I on Whitehall – and that statue is a great work of art too. And Gillian Wearing's Millicent Fawcett [p. 134] in Parliament Square is fantastic – especially its use of photographs.

'There's recently been a scramble for women artists, and I think this needs to include re-finding women who worked with men but were not credited. Ada almost fell out with Babbage because she wanted her name on the work. Men have tended to think of women as assistants.

'Etienne and I are a team, so this feels important. It's not always been easy to get both our names on work, and while nobody would dare ask Gilbert and George who did which bits, people do try to pick our partnership apart.

'We were commissioned to do Ada in early 2020. We borrowed the dress from the National Theatre

archive the day before it closed for the pandemic, and our daughter, trapped with us in lockdown, modelled for the statue.

'What next? We'd like to take inspiration from Proust's Veiled Wanderer and do a series of women wanderers: a Witch for Hackney, a Match-Girl for Spitalfields, a nun for Farringdon (where there was a convent) and a Prostitute for Piccadilly. Oh, and we'd like to do a statue of our former neighbour, Vivienne Westwood.'

Ada Salter

Ada Salter Bronze, 2014, with Dr Alfred Salter, their daughter Joyce and her cat (originally *Dr Salter's Dream*), 1991; moved to this location 2003, his statue recast in 2011–14 after it was stolen

By Diane Gorvin (b. 1956)

Bermondsey Wall East, SE16 4TZ (Thames Path, south bank, next to the Angel pub, opposite remains of Edward III Manor)

Also: a peaceful garden in nearby Southwark Park is named in Ada's honour.

Ada Salter (1866–1942) stands holding a spade, her other hand intended to carry live flowers (though it rarely does). Her emblem could hardly be anything else. To the distinction of being London's first elected female mayor – here in Bermondsey – she added the unprecedented greening of the entire borough and a key role in the creation of London's green belt.

Ada looks towards the Thames and the diminutive figure of Joyce, her only child, who died aged eight when an epidemic of scarlet fever swept through the slums where the family lived among the local poor they were working to help.

The loss devastated Ada and her doctor husband Alfred, but fuelled their drive to make Bermondsey a healthier place. And they did – improving housing and the environment, and promoting public health. Between 1911 and 1935 they are credited with cutting infant mortality by more than half, and almost eliminating perinatal maternal mortality. Small wonder they are local legends.

Ada and Alfred Salter plant a Tree of Heaven in Bermondsey.

Ada Brown joined the Methodist Bermondsey Settlement of Christian social reform volunteers in 1897. Here she met Alfred, a high-flying doctor who (to the annoyance of his commercially minded peers) charged his poverty-stricken patients just sixpence or nothing. They married in 1900, became Quakers and active socialists and in 1908 joined the new Labour Party. Ada encouraged the unionisation of working

women, campaigned for women's suffrage and fed the families of striking women in the 'Bermondsey Uprising' of 1911.

In 1914 she was elected National President of the Women's Labour League, and in 1922 became Mayor of Bermondsey. Which meant that when Alfred became Labour MP for Bermondsey West, the result was announced by . . . Ada.

The Salters pushed through a nationally admired slum clearance programme, and Ada designed an

estate of model council houses (with gardens, of course) that still stand on Wilson Grove. She believed strongly in the value of nature in improving physical and mental health. As mayor she planted thousands of trees in the borough – many of her favourite Tree of Heaven survive – and filled public spaces with colourful plants, playgrounds and community events. Her practice spread and led to urban beautification in many other places.

This installation originally showed Dr Salter dreaming of his lost child, but when his effigy was stolen (probably for scrap) in 2011, locals raised funds to replace it – and to add Ada Salter to the group. Not before time.

Agatha Christie Bronze, 2012

By Ben Twiston-Davies

Corner of Cranbourn St and Great Newport St, WC2H 7AB

With a suitably enigmatic half-smile, 'the Queen of Crime' looks out from the centre of a giant book. Agatha Christie (1890–1976) is not only the author of the world's most popular murder mysteries, but also the best-selling novelist of all time, having sold two billion books in 100 languages. Her memorial stands at the heart of London's theatreland because she also wrote the world's longest-running play.

Agatha Christie cuts *The Mousetrap* tenth anniversary cake.

The Mousetrap opened at the nearby Ambassadors Theatre in 1952, and still plays round the corner at St Martin's Theatre. This statue was unveiled in 2012 for the show's sixtieth anniversary and twenty-five-thousandth performance, and the eagle-eyed will spot a little mousetrap above Christie's head.

Born into an upper-middle-class family in Torquay, on Devon's 'English Riviera', Agatha Miller married army officer Archie Christie in 1914, and her only child, Rosalind, was born five years later. During both world wars Agatha Christie worked in hospital pharmacies, gleaning invaluable knowledge of poisons, which feature as means of murder in more than half her books.

Her first published novel, *The Mysterious Affair at Styles* (written to win a bet with her sister), came out in 1920, already featuring her punctilious refugee Belgian detective, Hercule Poirot, with his 'magnificent moustaches'. Spinster sleuth Miss Marple soon followed, and both are depicted on this monument.

Christie was, like her statue, neither notably non-conformist nor entirely conventional. She said in 1946 that she disliked crowds, loud noises, gramophones, cinemas, alcohol and smoking, adding, 'I do like sun, sea, flowers, travelling, strange foods, sports, concerts, theatres, pianos, and doing embroidery.' A keen swimmer, she is said to have been the first Western woman to surf standing up.

In 1926, already depressed after her mother's

death, Christie was left by her husband, and enthralled the world by disappearing. She was gone 11 days, before being found at a Harrogate hotel. It was her only mystery never neatly resolved.

After recuperating, Christie boarded the Orient Express (later the setting for *Murder on . . .*) to Istanbul and Baghdad, where she met the archaeologist Max Mallowan. They married in 1930, and their travels to his Middle Eastern excavations provided exotic locations for stories like *Death on the Nile* and *Appointment with Death*.

The 1950s saw Christie's work spread across stage and screen. She said writing plays was more fun than novels as it required no long descriptions. Soon she became the first, and so far only, woman to have three plays running simultaneously in London's West End.

Alison Lapper Pregnant Carrara Marble, 2005 (based on a 2000 cast)

By Marc Quinn

Fourth Plinth, Trafalgar Square 2005–7, various incarnations since. Not currently on view (we've made an exception for its inclusion here); in 2020 still seeking a permanent public home

See also: Interview with Alison Lapper (p. 20) and Fourth Plinth (p. 22)

Alison Lapper has congenital photomelia, and was born with no arms and very short legs. Institutionalised soon after birth, she had little family support, and came to reject the many mechanical limb replacements she was fitted with as unhelpful efforts to 'normalise' her. Determinedly herself, she overcame enormous odds to become an independent Mouth and Foot Painting Artist and, in 2000, mother of son Parys.

Lapper initially turned down Marc Quinn's request to sculpt her, suspicious of his motives. The second time he asked, she told him she was seven months pregnant. 'Even better,' he said. Surprised, she agreed to sit for him, and for two years (2005–7) the resulting 3.5m white marble statue looked down from the Fourth Plinth in Trafalgar Square (see p. 22). 'This sculpture gave me a voice for the first time,' she told the *Guardian*, 'and maybe it did the same for others who have different bodies. I was up there, a pregnant, naked, disabled single mother.'

Reaction varied – but was rarely neutral. The *Sun* ran the headline, 'Vulgar Trafalgar'. By contrast, the art critic Waldemar Januszczak wrote in the *Sunday Times* that the statue of Lapper, 'rhyming her physical shortenings with the Venus de Milo, must be ranked as one of the most significant sculptural moments in Britain's postwar art history'.

Few would now disagree that the statue – and the giant inflatable version of it that appeared at the opening ceremony of the London Paralympics (2012) – contributed to a turning point in attitudes to disability.

It is sad that this remarkable statue of an extraordinary woman is not on public view today; sadder still that it would now have painful added

Alison Lapper and son Parys at the unveiling of Marc Quinn's statue of her.

poignancy, as Parys died of a probably accidental drug overdose aged 19. His devastated mother pointed out that he was bullied at school about her disability and sectioned under the Mental Health Act two years before his death. This unbelievably resilient woman nonetheless wants to see the statue back on display.

Marc Quinn says the statue has been turned down across New York for being too controversial. But he is hopeful that one day, as a tribute to Alison, to Parys and 'as a celebration of motherhood and life, which relate universally', it will be returned to public view in London.

An Interview with Alison Lapper

How did you feel when the Fourth Plinth statue of you was unveiled in 2005?

I loved it. I kind of knew it wasn't going to go down as well as we hoped, but when my five-year-old son looked up at it and said, 'Mummy, you're beautiful,' I didn't care what anyone else thought.

It got a mixed reaction.

Mixed??! It was awful. 'Vulgar Trafalgar.' Disability? 'Ugly.' I can't believe that in this day and age we are still so uncomfortable with difference – that people are willing to be rude and aggressive to an individual just because their body is different.

Did the material – marble, a traditional stone for statues of status – make a difference?

Definitely. That was why Marc made it of marble. But I'm 'so important' that I'm now hidden away again under dustsheets. I may be in marble, but I'm not beautiful enough or acceptable enough, even in our 'progressive' society.

And the location in the square of 'heroes'?

Yes. Marc always said I was a heroine in my own right. I don't see myself that way, but with all that life has thrown at me and I'm still here – just – you do have to have some strength of character.

And everyone seems to forget that Nelson had only one arm and one eye (I've got two eyes!), but because he lost them in war, that's OK.

How much of a positive impact do you think your statue had on the public perception of disability?

I don't know if it did. If you've heard it did, that's good. At least it got people talking. But where am I now? It was, 'We'll be brave and do this, but then we'll put it away again.' Marc has been trying for twenty years to find a permanent public home for the statue, and he's still looking.

Is public art important?

Hugely. How are we going to change preconceived ideas if we don't make public art with something to say? But we need more that's controversial. If mine is one of the most controversial in twenty years that's a bit sad.

How do you feel about the statue now?

I still love it, and I'm proud of it. It is hard to look at since my beautiful boy died – now the worst thing that could possibly happen to me has happened – but it has made it into a memorial to him too. I still think it's beautiful – and the one Marc made when Parys was a few months old, with Parys sitting with me, is even more beautiful because my son is there. Marc gave me a maquette of that after Parys died.

I'd just like to see the statue out of the 'shameful' shadows and back in public – getting people talking, challenging ideas of beauty, and hopefully helping people get better at dealing with difference.

Alison Lapper at home with maquettes of the statues.

Females of the Fourth Plinth — from Alison Lapper Pregnant to Lady in Blue North-west corner, Trafalgar Square, WC2N 5DX

Named in 1830 for the 1805 naval victory against Napoleon, Trafalgar Square is dominated by military statuary. The hero of Trafalgar, Lord Nelson, stands so elevated he's hardly visible atop his 52m column (1840–4), while three of the four corner plinths support typical mid-nineteenth-century 'heroic' male figures. The fourth plinth (north-west corner) was intended to bear an equestrian statue of King William IV, to pair with his brother George IV (north-east corner), but money ran out and the plinth was left empty.

Since the 1990s a changing array of contemporary sculpture has been displayed here. Today the London Mayor's Fourth Plinth Programme claims (not unreasonably) to be 'probably the most famous public art commission in the world'. Selected works stand for up to two years and subject matter is open, though artists are asked to consider the context of Trafalgar Square.

The first formal commission certainly did – and challenged it. *Alison Lapper Pregnant* (2005) by Marc Quinn (b. 1964) celebrated, as he said, 'a different kind of heroism' and the 'different beauty' of a naked, pregnant, disabled woman. And instead of looking back like the square's other statues, it looked forward: 'pregnancy is about the future.' The work was controversial and important (more on p. 18-19).

Of the 13 mayoral commissions so far, four depict women, and five are by women. Notably, though, at the time of writing, the most recent five commissions (covering 2020–30) include four by women and two featuring women.

In 2009, Antony Gormley challenged the idea of putting statues on plinths. It implies a moral example or hero, he said, but 'we just don't believe in that any more . . . Everyone has moments of heroic fortitude.' His *One & Other* literally gave the plinth to one member of the public per hour 24 hours a day for 100 days. The 2,400 'plinthers', half of them women, could do whatever they liked: protest, perform or sit reading a book, creating a kind of collective portrait of early-twenty-first-century Britain.

A different kind of collective took the stand in 2024: Mexican artist Teresa Margolles' *Mil Veces un Instante, A Thousand Times in an Instant*, places nearly 800 life masks of UK- and Mexico-based trans/non-binary people in a *tzompantli* – a Mesoamerican skull rack traditionally used to display victims of war or sacrifice. A trained forensic pathologist, Margolles (b. 1963) has her studio in a Mexico City morgue. 'Looking at the dead', she says, 'you see society' – especially the victimised and marginalised,

Mil Veces un Instante

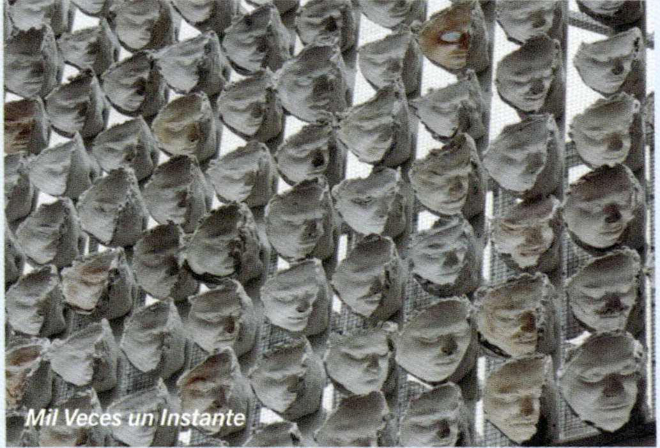

including her friend Karla, a trans woman whose 2015 murder remains unsolved.

The masks have a haunting quality. Facing inwards, their shadowy features seem to shift between concave and convex, and the detail is designed to deteriorate in the London weather.

A more joyful vision, *Lady in Blue* (2026, in maquette earlier) by the New York artist Tschabalala Self (b. 1990), depicts a self-possessed 'everywoman' of colour, striding confidently forward in a bright blue dress. Her bronze body invites comparison with the square's historic males, and the blue references the high-

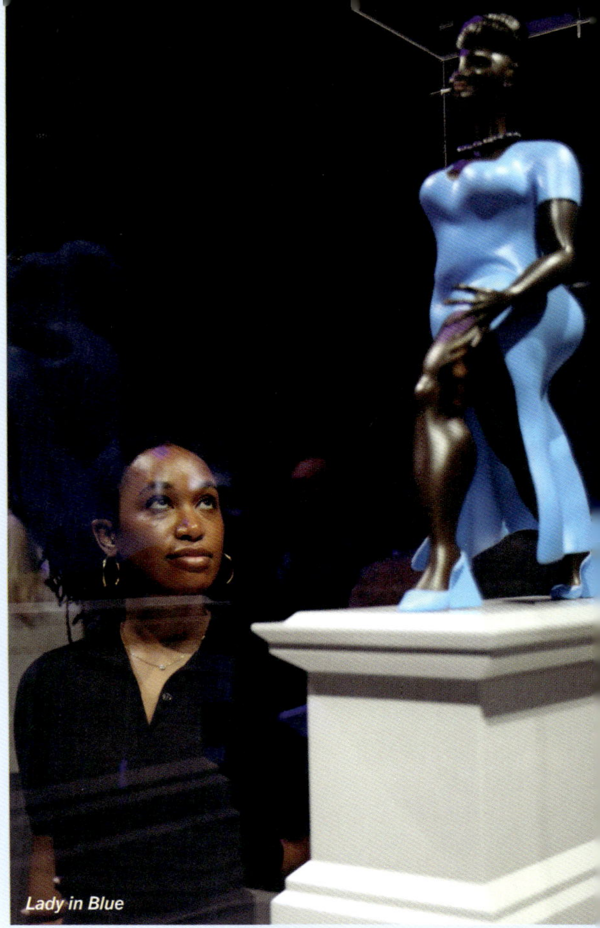
Lady in Blue

status Renaissance pigment lapis lazuli (often used for the Virgin Mary). Here it is for all of us, Self says, highlighting a quotidian icon symbolising 'our shared present and future'.

Amy Winehouse Bronze, 2014

By Scott Eaton
Stables Market, 407 Chalk Farm Road,
Camden, NW1 8AH

Amy Winehouse has not been put on a pedestal. One of Britain's most famous singer-songwriters stands among us, life-size and life-like. Her slight figure is lifted on high heels and extended by her signature beehive hairdo, but she can be quickly lost among market-goers and fans. People stop as if to chat, or place a protective, possessive arm around her shoulders (polishing them) for a photo.

The sculptor said he wanted to convey her 'attitude and strength, but also give subtle hints of insecurity'.

The childlike turned-in foot and hand fingering the hem of her skirt could look coy, but instead they hint at vulnerability. And she was vulnerable. After years of mental health problems and addiction,

Amy Winehouse performing at Koko in Camden just a mile from her statue.

Amy joined musical forebears from Jimi Hendrix to Janis Joplin in the notorious celebrity '27 Club', dying of alcohol poisoning weeks before her twenty-eighth birthday.

She lived and died nearby at 30 Camden Square. 'Amy was in love with Camden,' said her father Mitch Winehouse, so the family wanted her statue here, easily accessible and close to a favourite hangout, the Lock Tavern. Camden Council waived its usual rule that people must have been dead 20 years before a memorial, and Amy's statue was unveiled by her friend, actress Barbara Windsor, three years after she died.

Amy Jade Winehouse (1983–2011) grew up in London's Southgate, father a cabbie, mother a pharmacist, with jazz musicians in the family (grandmother Cynthia dated jazz club legend Ronnie Scott). Both parents are Jewish and, although Amy was not observant, she often wore a Star of David around her neck, as does her statue.

Amy's parents separated when she was nine. She attended stage school for a few years before dropping out at 16, working as an entertainment journalist and singing with the National Youth Jazz Orchestra and in clubs, until she signed her first artist's contract in 2002.

Her first album, *Frank* (2003), was a critical success, but it was her second album – sadly also her last – *Back to Black* (2006) that shot her to stardom. She was the first woman to win five Grammy Awards, with particular recognition for 'Rehab', a poignant song about her refusal to go into alcohol rehabilitation.

A P A N
R F T
M A
S T

The Awakening Bronze, 2002

By Unus Safardiar (b.1968)

St John's Lodge Garden, Inner Circle,
Regent's Park, NW1 4NR

Two faces, gently cocooned in an organic form, look tenderly into one another's eyes. It's genuinely touching, and surrounded by greenery in this peaceful garden built by Lord Bute in 1889 to be 'fit for meditation'.

I first took notice of this sculpture simply because I liked it. Then I read the dedication: 'In fond memory of Anne Lydia Evans (1929–99) who shared the secret of this garden'. Google eventually revealed this to be

Dr Anne Evans, a committed, socially conscious and forward-thinking local GP who had also worked for the Medical Foundation for the Care of Victims of Torture.

A moment of realisation: this was a memorial to a great friend of my mother's. The park authorities told me it had been commissioned by Mark Evans, whom I knew to be Anne's son. I tracked him down and we met for the first time in decades. Statues, it seems, hold histories and memories in many ways.

Anne Evans was not famous, but this contemplative piece of contemporary art commemorates a woman who had a positive impact on thousands of lives. Born Anne Jacobs into a Jewish family of medics in nearby Paddington, she followed the family profession, and in 1964 joined her mother and brother in their Marylebone surgery, where she stayed for 30 years. It was an innovative practice with its own mental health support (then very unusual), and Evans quickly gained a loyal following of patients, especially women.

She trained GPs, too, and amid the 1980s Lebanon war spent a year teaching family health at the American University in Beirut. After official retirement she used what the *British Medical Journal* called 'her compassion and fairness' to mediate between GPs and dissatisfied patients.

Anne came regularly to this garden from childhood, Mark told me – and brought her children often. She worked through her adolescent angst here ('her mother was too busy being a doctor'), and wheeled her newborn son here in his pram on his very first outing. It was here that Anne came to think and make life decisions, and here that Mark pushed her in her wheelchair in her final months. When she died, Mark wanted to give a sculpture to the garden in thanks for everything it had given his mother. Regent's Park said no; there was a ban on any further statuary. Mark got this byelaw lifted, and commissioned a suitable artwork – and Anne's meditative *Awakening* was quietly installed.

Anna Pavlova Gilded bronze. Original 1911, replacement copy 2006

High atop the cupola of this 1911 theatre, a golden Anna
Pavlova (1881–1931) balances on a single pointe. In
perfect equilibrium, she is nonetheless dynamic, the
prima ballerina mid-performance.

Born in St Petersburg, Russia, Pavlova was introduced
to London audiences in 1909 by the theatre impresario
Alfred Butt at the Palace Theatre (Cambridge Circus). Having built his own Victoria Palace venue,

Anna Pavlova performs 'The Dying Swan'.

designed by the great theatre architect Frank Matcham
(the Palladium, Coliseum, Hackney Empire), in 1911,
Butt not only presented this extraordinary dancer on its
stage, but also placed her shining effigy on its roof.

Despite its elegance, with taut muscles, swan neck
and proud face, Pavlova apparently considered looking
at her own statue to be bad luck and closed the curtains
of her carriage as she passed.

An unlikely star, Pavlova entered the Russian
Imperial Ballet School aged ten and was nicknamed
'the Broom' for her lanky legs and awkward ankles.
But she trained tirelessly and developed a particularly
expressive style. At 18 she joined the Imperial Ballet,
rising by 1906 to prima ballerina. Most famous for
'The Dying Swan', a solo created for her, she was
hugely popular. Her many fans were known, Swiftie-
style, as *Pavlovatzi*.

She worked briefly with Sergei Diaghilev at Ballet
Russe (refusing the lead in *The Firebird* because she
couldn't stand Stravinsky's music) before starting her
own company. Touring the world, from South Africa to
China, Pavlova added local dances (Mexican, Japanese,
Indian) to her repertoire along the way.

In 1912 she moved to London, settling at Ivy House
near Hampstead with her manager-husband and
various pets, including a swan. Two later statues of
her inhabit the garden here, but the house is now a
school with opaque fences. Pavlova died on tour in the

Hague and, despite Russian efforts to retrieve them, her ashes remain close to Ivy House in Golders Green Crematorium.

The name Pavlova still conjures the woman who was (and arguably is) the world's most famous ballerina, but also denotes a sweet, creamy, meringue-and-fruit pudding. This seems to have been named after her following Antipodean tours in the 1920s, but Australia and New Zealand still argue over who invented it.

As for the statue, eight years after Pavlova died, World War II began. Her figure was taken down for safe keeping – and lost. In 2006, photographs were used to recreate it and return Pavlova to her lofty spot, to glow again in golden arabesque.

Angela Burdett-Coutts Portland stone, 1865

Designed by Henry Astley Darbishire (1825–99)

Holly Village, Swain's Lane, N6 6QJ

The Neo-Gothic Baroness Burdett-Coutts Fountain in Victoria Park (E9 7DD) was also designed by Darbishire and funded by her 'for love of God and country'.

The Gothic saint-style figure of Angela Burdett-Coutts (1814–1906), a great Victorian philanthropist, stands to one side of the pretty arched entrance to the 12-house Neo-Gothic housing estate she built. To the other stands her governess-turned-lifelong-companion, Hannah Brown (née Meredith).

At the age of 23, Angela Burdett inherited staggering wealth from her step-grandmother, on several

conditions, including that she add her maternal grandfather's surname to her own. He was Thomas Coutts, co-founder of Coutts Bank, finance house to the rich and famous. Aged 80, he had married a young actress, Harriot Mellon, and Angela had been the only member of the family to offer her unreserved friendship. In due course Angela got the fortune.

It was a thoughtful bequest. Independent-minded and a committed Christian, 'Miss Coutts' refused numerous (inevitable) offers of marriage, instead living with Hannah (and for 11 years Hannah's husband, who was also Angela's doctor). Taking advice from Charles Dickens, she became known as 'Queen of the Poor' for her many effective welfare and education projects. There were carefully chosen one-off gifts too, including a clothes dryer sent to Florence Nightingale (p. 66) in the Crimea, and a fishing fleet bought for an impoverished Irish village.

Burdett-Coutts built churches and schools, co-founded what is now the NSPCC (National Society for the Prevention of Cruelty to Children), and was active in animal protection (note the little dog in her statue's arms).

In 1871 Queen Victoria made Coutts – unusually for a Victorian woman, entirely in her own right – Baroness Burdett-Coutts, while a year later she became the first woman to be awarded Freedom of the City of London in a ceremony at the Guildhall (p. 158).

Holly Village estate was her only fully commercial venture, the attractive houses rented at market rates. It was visible from her own Holly Lodge across the road, where Coutts lavishly entertained not only her many influential friends but also East End kids and contributors to societal good. At the age of 67 she risked all by 'scandalously' (and in contravention of the conditions of her legacy) marrying her assistant, 29-year-old William Bartlett. He proved a great support, and continued some of her work after her death. Only once both were gone was the Holly Lodge estate broken up and developed into the housing it is today. Holly Village – with its statues – survived intact.

Drinking Fountain Females

The drinking fountain colonisation of London began in 1859 with the founding of the Metropolitan Free Drinking Fountain Association by the Quaker MP (and nephew of reformer Elizabeth Fry) Samuel Gurney. It aimed to protect Londoners from the twin scourges of disease and alcoholism. Recent outbreaks of cholera that killed tens of thousands of people had been traced to London's polluted water (suppliers prioritising profits isn't new), and for the poor in particular the only safer alternative was beer or gin.

The fountains – numbering more than 500 by the end of the century – were increasingly eye-catching and sometimes propogandist. Where they featured figures, they were almost always women, seen as the givers of life, care and sustenance.

Funded by institutions, commerce and wealthy philanthropists (virtue signalling isn't new either), as well as by charities and public subscription, the fountains were often linked to the temperance movement, which campaigned against the social harms of alcohol.

Temperance drinking fountain, east side of road at north end of Blackfriars Bridge, (since 1911). Bronze, 1861. By Wills Bros.

Temperance drinking fountain, NE edge of Clapham Common (near the Tube) since 1895. Bronze figures by August von Kreling, architect Charles Barry Jnr.

An early flagship, donated by Gurney himself, the *Temperance fountain* now at Blackfriars has lost the elaborate canopy it sported when first placed (after much argument) outside the City's Royal Exchange in 1861. But it retains its bronze personification of Temperance, scantily clad in classical drapery and holding a water vase. Variations on this theme – classical woman with water vessel – soon proliferated.

The *Temperance Fountain on Clapham Common* has the young woman more comprehensively clothed, her pretty face beneath a headscarf. Her pitcher is rather small, but she seems to have quenched the thirst of the disabled man beside her. First installed at London Bridge, the fountain was so heavy that it did structural damage to warehouses below and had to be moved. In Clapham, decades later it became – ironically – something of a gathering point for alcoholics.

The *Whiting Fountain* at the City's Guilford Place, one of the few restored to working order, was donated by the Whiting sisters in memory of their mother or father, and depicts a serene-looking 'woman of

Samaria' kneeling with a water jug. According to the Bible, Jesus met the woman at a well. Having engaged with her despite the enmity between Jews and Samaritans (and her five ex-husbands), Jesus converted her to Christianity. 'Whosoever drinketh of this water shall thirst again,' he told her, 'but whosoever drinketh of the water I shall give him shall never thirst' (John IV 13–14, King James version) – a biblical verse that appeared on multiple temperance-linked drinking fountains.

Sometimes mistaken for a woman of Samaria, the semi-naked *Fountain Nymph* in Berkeley Square is more sensual than most of her biblical counterparts. She was sculpted by an associate of the Pre-Raphaelites, who almost certainly intended (favourable) comparison with Temperance figures. Certainly, an engraving made of the Nymph when the fountain was installed (1867), reproduced on the square's information board, does nothing to play

Whiting Fountain, Guilford Place, Holborn, WC1N 1EA. Marble, c.1870. By Henry Darbishire (1825–99).

Fountain Nymph, south end of Berkeley Square, W1. Carrara marble (on red granite), 1867.
By Alexander Munro.

down its 'tits' (see p. 100) eroticism.

There were other themes. The City's *La Maternité Charity Drinking Fountain* was deliberately different. Taking the idea of feminine sustenance to its natural conclusion, it depicts a breastfeeding mother (Charity) in contemporary clothes, her bountiful boob exposed. Its 1878 installation prompted a letter to the *Globe* newspaper. Should not the neighbouring statue of philanthropist George Peabody 'be turned', asked the (male) correspondent, until the 'lacteal sustentation' be completed or the mother provided by the sponsoring Company of Drapers and Merchant Taylors with more clothes? He seems, thankfully, to have had his tongue in his cheek, and when the statues were reconfigured in the 1980s it was not for this reason.

Also erected in 1878, the *Matilda (or St Pancras) Drinking Fountain* in Camden shows an idealised rural young woman (often called a milkmaid) looking into the distance. The plaque tells us it was donated by

La Maternité, Charity Drinking Fountain, Royal Exchange Avenue, EC3V 3NL. 1879 original in marble, replaced in 1897 with bronze. By Jules Dalou (1838–1902).

Matilda, wife of Richard Kent Esq., Junior Church Warden. Junior warden maybe, but they – or she – must have had money. Documents show this fountain cost £200 – equivalent to more than £30,000 today.

London's nineteenth-century drinking fountains were hugely popular. Charles Dickens wrote in 1879 that 'It is estimated that 300,000 people take advantage of the fountains on a summer's day' – and they did help improve health. So it is sad that so few survive, and that even those that do are almost all dry. This includes the city's only *Wallace Fountain* – despite more than 100 Wallace Fountains functioning in Paris.

The first 50 were donated to the French capital in 1872 by Sir Richard Wallace (1818–90), the illegitimate half-brother or son (nobody knows which) of the Marquis of Hertford, who left him huge wealth and his exceptional art collection (core of London's Wallace Collection). Resident in Paris and seeing the same problems as in London, Wallace sketched the initial design himself, wanting the fountains to be practical, scalable and attractive.

Four caryatids (holding up an ornate protective dome) prevented horses from nosing the constantly flowing water, while allowing human hands to reach through and fill a cup. The female figures personify four virtues: kindness, simplicity, charity and, of course, sobriety (though as they lack attributes, it's unclear which is which). There are well over 200 Wallace Fountains worldwide; the London one was cast after Wallace's death and erected in Shoreditch in 1904. When it stopped working the Wallace Collection asked to have it, and in 1960 it was installed here.

The organisation that kicked all this off in 1859 still exists as the Drinking Fountain Association, helping to restore historic fountains and add occasional new ones. However, with Londoners buying some two billion plastic water bottles a year, a different kind of pollution crisis prompted a new drinking fountain colonisation in 2024, with the Mayor's office leading the installation of 100 twenty-first-century water fountains/filling stations. The water is welcome – pity no new statues come with it.

Wallace drinking fountain. Outside Wallace Collection, Manchester Square, W1U 3BN (since 1960). Cast iron, painted green; designed 1872, cast 1904. By Charles-August Lebourg (1829–1906).

Diana Drinking Fountain Green Park, W1J 9DZ (just outside Tube exit). By Estcourt J. Clack (1906–73), bronze, 1954, restored and moved here 2011. Unusually sponsored by a fund for art, not temperance, this lithe naked huntress – Roman Diana, Greek Artemis – depicts a contradictory figure. She was invoked in Ancient times by women seeking fertility and safe childbirth – an odd role for a virgin hunter. In Ovid's *Metamorphoses* she turns fellow hunter Actaeon into a deer and sees him ripped to death by his dogs. His crime? *Accidentally* seeing her skinny-dipping. Diana also appears on a (non-drinking) fountain nearby in Hyde Park Rose Garden (1899, bronze) by Feodora Gleichen, the first woman to be elected a member of the Royal Society of British Sculptors – sadly just after her death in 1922..

Peace Memorial Drinking Fountain Smithfield Rotunda Garden, EC1A 9DY. Bronze and stone, 1873. Architect Frances Butler, sculptor John Birne Philip.
A female personification of Peace (see also p. 197) takes centre stage on this large, once-elaborate drinking fountain. She has lost her Gothic canopy and female companions Temperance, Faith, Hope and Charity, but she stands tall, classically draped, blessing us with one hand while holding an olive branch in the other. The fountain was paid for by a legacy left more than three centuries earlier by Elizabeth I's jeweller, goldsmith and Lord Mayor of London, Martin Bowes, for the maintenance of water conduits. Since the conduits had been replaced, the City Corporation saw fit to spend the accumulated £1,200 (about £165,000 today) on a fancy drinking fountain.

Henry Shrubsole Memorial Drinking Fountain Market Place, Kingston-upon-Thames, KT1 1JT. Carrara marble (on granite), 1882. By Francis John Williamson (1833–1920).
Local people raised £500 towards this classic drinking fountain In Kingston marketplace to commemorate Henry Shrubsole, banker and thrice mayor of Kingston, who expired suddenly in 1880 in the middle of a dinner for the poor. A drinking fountain must have seemed an appropriate memorial, both monumental and benevolent to the many locals who lacked any other source of safe water.

Edward VII Jewish Memorial Drinking Fountain Whitechapel Rd, E1 1DB (just west of Whitechapel Station, often surrounded by the market). Bronze on granite, 1911. By William Silver Frith (1850–1924).
Three allegorical women adorn this undeservedly ignored drinking fountain often surrounded by the detritus of the local market. It was paid for by Jewish East Enders, and inaugurated by Charles Rothschild in 1912 in memory of the just-late king. An female angel of peace blesses us from above, flanked by winged female personifications of Liberty, with an attractive contemporary face, and a sterner Justice (see also p. 90). Beneath each, putti hold items important to the local Jewish community: cloth (most were employed in the garment trade), a book (education/the Talmud), a ship (migration) and a car (future/technology). The memorial was the brainchild of Jewish writer Annie Gertrude Landa, whose journalist husband had scooped the death of the king having found himself on a telephone crossed line with the then Home Secretary Winston Churchill.

Anne of Bohemia and Catherine de Valois

Stone, 1879–80s and 1980s re-carving

By Nathaniel Hitch (1845–1938), designed by Sir George Gilbert Scott (1811–78) with 1980s restoration

Either side of the north door (Anne & Richard II left, Catherine and Henry V right) of Westminster Abbey facing Parliament Square, SW1 3PA

Flanking the north door of Westminster Abbey are two queens consort of England, Catherine de Valois (1401–37) alongside Henry V and Anne of Bohemia (1366–94) with Richard II. Both couples were crowned and buried inside the abbey – which they also both helped to construct.

Anne was the daughter of Holy Roman Emperor King Charles IV of Bohemia, who ruled half of Europe's population. She grew up mostly at Prague Castle, and in 1382 married Richard II in Westminster Abbey. Teenage pawns in the labyrinthine religious politics of the time, they nonetheless became a devoted couple.

On arrival in England Anne was abused for bringing no dowry but, despite remaining childless (which might then have elicited more abuse), she became increasingly popular. By the time she died aged 28, probably of the plague, she was popularly known as 'Good Queen Anne'.

Certainly her husband was a more successful king while she lived. After her death, he tried to secure peace with France by marrying the seven-year-old French princess Isabella de Valois, but within three years had been deposed by his cousin and quickly died. The cousin became Henry IV.

Peace with France didn't last either. Henry IV's son Henry V is best known for his victory at Agincourt

– hence his depiction here in battle dress. He too attempted a French diplomatic marriage (in 1420), to Isabella's younger sister, Catherine de Valois. Henry was soon back off to campaign in France, however, leaving his pregnant wife behind, and in 1422 he died of dysentery, never seeing his baby son, the future Henry VI.

A widow at 21, Catherine went on to marry (or possibly not marry – it was highly contentious) the Welsh squire Owen Tudor, producing six children and founding the Tudor dynasty through her grandson Henry VII.

The construction of his ornate Lady Chapel in Westminster Abbey led to his grandmother's body being moved. Her damaged coffin left her visible for the next 270 years, and in 1669 the diarist Samuel Pepys was thrilled to visit and "kiss a queen". Finally re-interred in 1778, Catherine was only properly reburied in Victoria's reign, appropriately in the Henry V Chapel.

This was the idea of the abbey's Victorian surveyor, the architect Sir George Gilbert Scott, who was also responsible for the figures of Catherine standing demurely beside her first husband, and Anne alongside hers, that we see adorning the abbey today.

Anne of Denmark Portland stone, completed 1672

Temple Bar; almost certainly designed by Christopher Wren (1632–1723); statues by John Bushnell (1636–1701)

Paternoster Square, EC4M 7DX, since 2004

See also: Temple Bar Memorial, featuring Queen Victoria and a miniature of this statue (p. 156)

Anne of Denmark (1574–1619), wife of King James I (VI of Scotland), peers down at modern Paternoster Square, her back to St Paul's Cathedral. A little worse for wear (she is 350 years old and much travelled), Queen Anne graces Temple Bar, once the most prestigious gateway into the City of London. Originally standing where Fleet Street meets the Strand, Anne looked down on massed traffic and occasional royal processions en route from Westminster to St Paul's.

The other seven City gates were demolished in the eighteenth century (including Ludgate – see p. 156), but Temple Bar survived until 1878, when it was replaced with the Temple Bar Memorial. The seventeenth-century gateway was preserved, its stones carefully stored, before being reconstructed at a private estate in Hertfordshire. Here it remained until the City claimed it back in the early 2000s to rebuild it once more.

Commissioned by Charles II, the gate features him and his father Charles I on one side, and on the other his grandparents, James and Anne. The Danish princess was married to James VI of Scotland in 1589 at 14. Her arrival was months delayed by storms, and in the end James sailed to Norway to collect her in what a 1950s biographer called the one romantic episode of his life.

Initially they got on well, despite rumours that he preferred men. The relationship suffered, however, from a near-decade-long custody battle over their firstborn son. King James, following tradition, sent Henry to be raised by a trusted earl; Anne fought tooth and nail to get him back. She finally succeeded when James acceded to the English throne in 1603 and the family, including nine-year-old Henry, moved south.

Viewed suspiciously by some of Scotland's puritanical Presbyterians, this vivacious young queen

was freer in London. She became a noted patron of the arts, commissioning lavish masques, in which she sometimes performed. Often written by the playwright Ben Jonson, they were designed by Inigo Jones – soon to be the architect of the new masque-friendly banqueting hall at Whitehall Palace.

Having watched the teenage Henry die in 1612, Anne fortunately did not live to see her younger son, Charles I, beheaded outside this same building. She would, though, I think, have enjoyed the exuberant Restoration theatre – and resulting rise of female actors (see p. 176) – encouraged by his son, her grandson, who erected this statue.

Boadicea and her Daughters Bronze, 1856–83; erected 1902

By Thomas Thornycroft

North side of Westminster Bridge (close to Westminster Tube station), SW1A 2JH

Boudica or Boudicca ('Boadicea' was the Victorian locution) pilots a scythed war chariot drawn by powerful rearing horses and brandishing a spear . . . wearing what looks like a semi-transparent negligée.

Dramatic and dynamic, this statue of the first-century warrior queen of Ancient Britain rides high above a tourist kiosk at the end of Westminster Bridge, surrounded by crowds staring up at Big Ben.

This is a Victorian Boudica, almost a Brittanica, appropriated for an imperial Britain led by a female monarch. Prince Albert was involved with its design, lending his horses as models, and it has even been suggested that Boudica resembles the young Victoria. The nineteenth-century queen's name of course means 'victory', and linguists have suggested that 'Boudica'

Boudica enlisted for the Votes for Women campaign.

also derives from the Celtic for 'victorious woman'.

Boudica's two daughters ride either side of her, breasts bare. Some excuse for their semi-nakedness can perhaps be found in their prior fate, which their mother is riding into war partly to avenge.

Boudica's husband, Prasutagus, King of the Iceni (in modern Norfolk), had treatied with Rome. But when he died around 60 AD, the historian Tacitus

tells us, the Romans – who had little time for female leadership – pillaged Iceni land, whipped Boudica and raped her daughters.

Allying with a neighbouring tribe, the Trinovantes (of Essex), Boudica led a massive revolt, sacking the Roman capital Camulodunum (Colchester), then Londinium (London) and Verulamium (St Albans). She killed some 70–80,000 men, women and children (classical sources say), before finally being defeated by the Roman army and dying, possibly by her own

hand, before she could be captured.

The Victorians aren't the only ones to have appropriated her story. Boudica was popular in Renaissance England, when another female monarch, Elizabeth I, led the nation against invasion (the Spanish Armada). The ancient queen continued to grow in the popular imagination as a symbol of Anglo independence and power, appearing in plays, poetry and visual arts.

Thomas Thornycroft began this statue, his magnum opus, in the 1850s, but only in 1902 was it erected here, just in time for the coronation of Edward VII (see also p.35 and 197). Perfect timing, too, for Boudica to be appropriated once more – by the Suffragettes, themselves now memorialised on the other side of Parliament (p. 134).

Britannia See also: Ladies of the Bank (p.80)

Britannia made her debut two millennia ago as one of several Classical female personifications of places that were seen not merely as emblems but as protectors and legitimisers of (usually male) rulers. Britannia began as brand management and has remained so, through various rebrands, ever since.

A robust female personification of the nation, usually militarily apparelled in helmet and shield, spear or trident in hand, she is first seen on Roman coins, a warrior goddess representing the Roman province of Britannia. She was akin to Roma, the female personification of Rome, and Roma in turn was probably modelled on Athena, protector of Athens. As the Greek goddess of wisdom and strategic war, Athena was the precursor of the Roman goddess Minerva – who also shares attributes with Britannia (see also p. 42).

Rome didn't mind presenting Britannia as strong – that showed how strong it was for subduing her. This naturally also meant that she was ripe for adoption by a later independent Britain that idolised the classical world and sought to

Roman sestertius 140–4 AD with Britannia on it.

project its own power.

Britannia first appeared on British coins in the reign of Charles II (1660–85), and her role as a figure of national unity was amplified after the Act of Union (1707) that merged England and Scotland into Great Britain. This happened under a female monarch, Queen Anne (p. 152), and a pattern coin (never circulated) was made with a recognisable Anne as Britannia.

The patriotic song 'Rule, Britannia!' ('Britannia rule the waves') was written in 1740, and in 1797 numismatic Britannia swapped her spear for a trident, referencing Roman/Greek sea god Neptune/Poseidon in recognition of the importance of the Royal Navy. Following Nelson's naval victory over Napoleon at the Battle of the Nile in 1799, the sculptor John Flaxman designed a colossal 230-foot (70m) statue of Britannia for Greenwich Hill. It was never made, but many smaller figures of Britannia followed.

Britannia got a major boost under Queen Victoria and the person and personification merged more than ever. Britannias bloomed on all sorts of public buildings, from the Foreign Office to the fish market – anything governmental or commercial claiming national status. The originally Roman personification of Britain was a perfect symbol for the powerful, female-led global British Empire that outstripped even that of Rome.

Britannias about Town

Britannia and France on Queen Anne's statue

By Frances Bird, 1712, but this is an 1886 copy (see p. 152)

St Paul's Cathedral steps

Britannia holds the side of the royal coat of arms. On the other side of it sits France – but her hand does not touch it. When this statue was first erected, Britain had just made peace with France after more than a decade at war. France wears a military helmet. Britannia wears a laurel wreath, symbol of victory.

Britannia tops this war memorial arch commemorating the 585 staff of the station who died 'for their country' in the First World War (yes, 585 from a single railway company). The remaining staff were apparently consulted about the design, and to the left of the arch is an unusually visceral depiction of war with a vicious-looking war goddess Bellona. To the right a group representing peace centres on Athena holding a statue of Nike, goddess of victory (see p. 194). Above them both, Britannia holds her trident in one hand and with the other raises aloft a flame of liberty.

Mirror images of a tall upright Britannia stand at the southern corners of this major 1920s commercial building designed by Edwin Lutyens (1869–1944) for the Anglo-Persian Oil Company, later BP. With an Art Deco face, classical drapery, union flag shield and her foot on a small globe, the iconography here is full-on colonial. Britannia is accompanied (on the Finsbury Circus façade) by a topless female Persian scarf dancer, a male Indian water carrier and a rather lovely fully clothed (non-British) woman with baby.

Britannia, Somerset House

Architect: James Pennethorne, sculpture, William Theed, except London by James Legrew, 1856.

West facade 'New Wing' overlooking Lancaster Place (Waterloo Bridge approach)

In the 1770s London was felt to have insufficient statement public buildings compared with other European capitals (like Paris), so Somerset House was built in 1775 (replacing a crumbling royal palace) with the clear purpose of embodying national pride. What could be more appropriate than adding

– albeit in a later phase of building – an archetypal Britannia atop a street-facing pediment? And she is not the only female personification of place here. Beneath her stand figures representing six cities – Belfast, Dublin, Edinburgh, Glasgow, London and Manchester – all wearing mural crowns, coronets of city walls, classically marking their protective role.

Tate Britain Britannia

Architect: Sidney Smith, 1897.

Atop the art gallery, Millbank, SW1P 4RG.

Not the usual stern Britannia, this one has a rather sweet young face (though you need binoculars or a zoom to see it) – perhaps appropriate to an arts rather than military or government building.

Britannia seated on a lion, County Fire Office (and Alliance Life) building

By Hermon Cawthra (1886–1971).

50 Regent St, Piccadilly Circus, W1B 5RL. Stone, mid-1920s, but similar to one it replaced dating to 1819.

See also his *Mother and Child*, p. 147)

A classic imperial Britannia with all the usual attributes and the union flag on her shield. The lion – a not uncommon addition – is a symbol of England, royalty and, of course, courage.

The traditional Britannia that sits high on the roof above the entrance to the FCDO is in fact Queen Victoria as Britannia. Her sceptre is broken – not a great look for British diplomacy – but otherwise she is the ultimate national representative, merging monarch and myth, person and personification. Her four standing rooftop companions are female figures of (L–R): Legislation (holding paper), Wisdom (with a book), Justice with sword and scales (see also p. 90) and Navigation (with a rudder).

   Next door is another 'Britannia' – actually intended to symbolise Government. She sits at the centre of the pediment above the door to 100 Parliament Street – always government offices. With the face of a young Edwardian, she is flanked by semi-naked male and female personifications of law and order, and various aspects of education, trade and industry.

A conventional seated Victorian Britannia.

Flanking the door to what was once the Peninsula & Oriental (P&O) booking office, a splendid pair of caryatids represents the two ends of the shipping line: Britain and 'the Orient'. The contrast is interesting: the

Eastern figure is soft-robed, with beads round her neck and smiling. Britannia is hard-faced, and helmeted with a breast plate bearing the three lions emblem of England. But then Britain had just emerged from the First World War. Indeed, P&O were only here because this building, constructed in 1906 for a German shipping company, had been seized as reparations. There is an unusual female personification of Germany high up on the right-hand façade of the building.

George Gilbert Scott designed this impressive 1868 Victorian Gothic building, with a row of niches for statuary, but budget cuts left the building with only one: this lonely rooftop Britannia who stands silhouetted against the sky looking rather out of place. She sports a visible trident and apparently is also a lightning conductor, so she is at least defending the building.

Bronze Woman Bronze, 2008

By Ian Walters (1930–2006) and Aleix Barbat

Stockwell Memorial Garden, SW8 1UQ

Also of note: The mural next to the statue includes a memorial to Violette Szabo (see p. 200), who grew up in nearby Burnley Rd; there is a plaque on Cécile Nobrega's Stockwell home, 10 Nealden Street, SW4 9QX.

Regularly cited as the first statue of a black woman in London (and England) – it isn't (see p. 50). The figure of young Joy Battick (p. 86) up the road at Brixton Railway Station predates it by more than two decades. But that is not to detract from this joyful statue, which was the first to consciously honour women of

Cécile Nobrega with Bronze Woman

Caribbean heritage.

It is based on a poem of the same name by the Stockwell-based poet, musician, teacher and campaigner Cécile Nobrega (1919–2013). She grew up in Guyana, and came to the UK in 1969 with her husband and three children. Here she continued to teach, write and compose, and became active in the National Union of Teachers and several social action organisations.

The poem was published in her first book of poetry in 1968 when she was still in Guyana. It is about Caribbean motherhood, slave motherhood ('when you laid with massa boss, free or forced') and universal motherhood. And so is the statue.

The Bronze Woman stands barefoot in a simple dress and head-wrap, eyes locked lovingly with those of her child whom she holds aloft – lifting up the next generation. As the poem says:

> *Strength sweat and toil,*
> *who can foil*
> *your quest*
> *for best*
> *to give your child?*

And it ends with a call to honour the contribution – often against the odds – of Caribbean mothers.

> *Who can help but cherish*
> *This monument of Love . . .*
> *Then find me a place in the sun*
> *in the sea*
> *on a rock*

Near an Isle
In the Caribbee: There I will set her,
Bronze Woman, Free
Honoured for shaping Our Destiny.

By the time the monument finally materialised the poem was 50 years old, and Nobrega had been campaigning for the statue for a decade. It was designed by Ian Walters, who sculpted the Nelson Mandela in Parliament Square, but completed after his death by a London art student.

The statue was finally unveiled in 2008 by a circle of Caribbean-heritage women, including Doreen Lawrence and Baroness Howells, for the sixtieth anniversary of the arrival of the *Empire Windrush* and the two-hundredth anniversary of the end of legal slavery.

Bronze Woman stands not in the Caribbean sun and sea but on a small patch of grass surrounded by traffic, just north of Stockwell Tube. Sadly, this Caribbean mother is still getting less attention and recognition than she deserves.

Chronology of Statues of Colour

One thing is clear: monuments to women of colour have been slow in coming. Less clear is which can legitimately claim to be first. Even respectable sources credit at least four different statues as the first public effigy of a woman of colour in London. What's going on?

The confusion is mostly down to definitions of 'black' and 'of colour', and the loss of caveats that would make the claims accurate.

Statues of women of colour have in fact existed on the streets of London since the eighteenth century, with several appearing on prominent monuments and public buildings (the Albert Memorial, the Foreign Office), but these are symbolic caricatures personifying Africa and Asia and we aren't including them here.

As far as I can ascertain, the chronology and 'firsts' are as follows:

1. 1986: Joy Battick (p. 86), black Brixton resident, arrives in full-length, life-size bronze at Brixton railway station as part of a three-statue installation, *Platforms Piece*. She is not named on the installation, but she is certainly real.

The first statue of a real woman of colour in London.

2. 1998: Manche Masemola, a black South African girl, and Esther John (birth name Qamar Zia), a Pakistani missionary, are commemorated with full-length stone statues (each in its own niche) as part of a group of ten 'Modern Martyrs' on the façade of Westminster Abbey (p. 132).

The first statues of individually identified women of colour. Masemola is the first named black woman of colour, Zia the first named Asian woman, and also the first real Asian woman.

3. 2008: Bronze Woman – a generic but naturalistic black woman (and child) inspired by a poem of the same name is erected in Stockwell, celebrating Afro-Caribbean women.

The first solo statue (i.e. not part of a group) of a naturalistic woman of colour in London.

4. 2012 (November): Noor Inayat Khan (p. 142), a half-Indian war heroine, is commemorated with a

standalone bust in Gordon Square.

The first solo monument to a named woman of colour/ woman of Asian heritage.

5. 2013: Nicola Adams (p. 182), the black British Olympic gold-medal-winning boxer, is installed with two men on a Sustrans Portrait Bench in Downhills Park, Tottenham, in the form of a 2D metal cut-out.

6. 2016: Mary Seacole (p. 126 and 184), a half-Jamaican Crimean War nurse, is celebrated with a striking, larger-than-life statue outside St Thomas' Hospital.

This statue is frequently named as the first. It is in fact the first solo statue of a real, named black (as opposed to Asian) woman, and the first full-length solo statue of a real named woman of colour.

These are only the 'firsts'. In recent years more statues of women of colour have arrived. The Windrush generation has been commemorated with the National Windrush Memorial (p. 208) and Hackney's Warm Shores (p. 206). While *Joy Battick II* (this time named) has joined her earlier statue at Brixton Station.

Catherine Booth Bronze, 1929

By George Edward Wade (1853–1933)

William Booth Training College, Champion Park, SE5 8BQ

See also: Copy in fibreglass (2015, for Salvation Army's hundred-and-fiftieth anniversary) at Tower Hamlets Mission, 31 Mile End Rd, Tower Hamlets, E1 4TP
NB: contrary to appearances, the public is welcome in the building, where there is a small public museum.

As you emerge from Denmark Hill Station, a vast tower looms, adorned with a huge white cross. A domineering 1929 creation of Giles Gilbert Scott (with similarities to his power stations at Battersea and Bankside – now Tate Modern), this is the Salvation Army's training centre. In front stand two larger-than-life bronze figures. Founder and first 'General'

William Booth (1829–1912) has his arm raised in declaration and benediction, while his wife, 'Army Mother' Catherine Booth (1829–90), holds her hand open in invitation. It's a revealing difference.

Catherine was born into a religious temperance household (though to her consternation, her father later returned to drinking), and campaigned against alcohol from the age of 14. She met William when he spoke at her South London church, and in 1855 they married, travelling the country as he, and soon (despite initial nervousness) she also, preached.

In 1859 Catherine wrote her first pamphlet, 'Female Teaching', responding to a clergyman who declared that a visiting American Methodist, Phoebe Palmer, should not, as a woman, be preaching. Nonsense, argued Catherine cogently, adding that the 'unjustifiable application' of St Paul's exhortation, 'Let your women keep silent in

the churches,' had resulted in 'loss to the church, evil in the world, and dishonour to God'. Soon Catherine was a more popular preacher than her husband.

In 1865 they launched their Christian Mission in the East End, reorganised in 1878 as the Salvation Army. Its primary purpose was, and remains, 'the saving of souls', but they soon recognised that hunger impeded spiritual engagement, and became involved in social work: 'soup, soap, salvation'.

Catherine campaigned against the sexual

exploitation of girls, contributing to the raising of the age of consent in 1885 to 16. It was also she who introduced the Sally Army's signature music, adapting popular songs and convincing William that the Devil should not have all the best tunes.

She ensured that women held Army office from the start, but this was Victorian England, and on marriage their pay went to their husbands. Only in the 1960s was Catherine fully credited as co-founder.

When Catherine died from breast cancer aged 61 – or in Sally Army parlance 'was promoted to glory' – 30,000 lined the funeral route. William lived another 22 years before the oldest of their eight children, Bramwell, succeeded. He was followed by his sister Evangeline, the first of three female Generals to date in this still-thriving evangelical and charitable organisation.

Dancer with Ribbon Bronze, 1997

By Michael Rizzello (1926–2004)

120–22 Oxford St (above Next on north side of street), W1D 1LT

And: *Young Dancer* (bronze); by Enzo Plazzotta (1921–81). Erected 1988 by arrangement between Westminster City Council and his estate. Broad Court (Bow St end, diagonally opposite the Royal Opera House), WC2B 5QH.
See also: Anna Pavlova (p. 28), Millbank, SW1 (bronze, 1975).

Above Oxford Street's shoppers a dynamic young dancer with a swirling ribbon looks as if she is about

to prance right across the street at Christmas lights level. The movement is joyous, and has an abandon that, along with its very young face and top-of-the-head ponytail, makes this look more like a child than the top ballerina, Darcy Bussell, on whom it is apparently based.

Oddly enough, another statue,

Darcey Bussell performs a Pas de Deux.

Young Dancer, opposite the Royal Opera House where Bussell performed from the age of 17, seems more representative of Bussell. Here a sinuous ballerina sits, hair in a bun, concentrating on lacing her pointe shoes as if preparing for practice, with a focus Bussell must have had to reach the heights she did.

Bussell was born Marnie Mercedes Darcy Pemberton Crittle in London in 1969. Her father was an Australian fashion designer who didn't stick around, her mother a model who soon re-married, giving Darcy a new father, dentist Philip Bussell.

Despite starting serious training 'late' (she joined the Royal Ballet School at 13) and being 'too tall' for a ballerina (1.7m), at 20 Bussell became the youngest-ever principal at the Royal Ballet. In 1997, the year the Oxford Street statue was made, she married

Australian hedge-fund
manager Angus Forbes and,
to be fair to the sculptor,
there are photos from this
time in which she does look
very young.

In a phenomenal act of
determination that made
ballet history, Bussell returned
to her principal role(s) after
giving birth to each of her
two daughters – both born
by Caesarean section. She
retired from the Royal Ballet
aged 37 in 2007 after 20 years
with the company, her body
(unsurprisingly) rebelling.

But the obsessiveness
required for such a role
doesn't disappear overnight.
She still danced – including
for the 2012 London Olympics
opening ceremony – and
has gone on to coach, write
books, campaign for dance
in schools, and judge *Strictly
Come Dancing*. So perhaps the
youthful dynamism of the
little *Dancer with Ribbon* is not
so inappropriate after all.

Diana, Princess of Wales Bronze, 2021

By Ian Rank-Broadley (b. 1952)
Sunken Garden, Kensington Palace,
Kensington Gardens, W8 4PX

After her 'fairytale' wedding to Prince Charles (now King Charles III) in 1981 – watched by 750 million people – Princess Diana (1961–97) lived at Kensington Palace for 15 years. On the twentieth anniversary of her death, her sons William and Harry commissioned this memorial statue for the palace garden and unveiled it on what would have been their mother's sixtieth birthday.

Critical response was mixed. Some loved it. Jonathan Jones of the *Guardian* (known for trenchant reviews) had hoped for something 'provocative' but found it 'joyless . . . spiritless . . . nonsense'. And the princes clearly weren't aiming for innovative art. The statue is intended to evoke their mother and, apart from the far-too-masculine face, it does.

Born into the aristocracy, Diana Spencer spent her childhood on the royal Sandringham estate, playing with Princes Andrew and Edward and calling the queen 'Aunt Lilibet'. Her childhood was unhappy and unstable – her words – as she and her siblings suffered from their parents' acrimonious divorce and remarriages.

Diana met Prince Charles, 12 years her senior, when she was 16 and he was dating her older sister.

Three years later, he proposed. At the time, Diana (having failed her school exams) was working as a nursery school assistant. She always loved children – hence the three with her in this statue (London's first of the princess), and the nature of her two previous memorials in this park, the Diana playground and the Diana Fountain (and paddling pool).

Diana tried to give her sons some childhood 'normality', but soon they too were afflicted by parental acrimony. In 1986 Diana had an affair and

Charles resumed his relationship with Camilla Parker-Bowles (now the Queen). Things got steadily worse, and more public. Divorce in 1996 saw the fairytale turn full nightmare a year later when Diana was killed in a car crash in Paris with her boyfriend, Dodi Fayed, while being pursued by paparazzi. Her young sons had to walk behind their mother's coffin in a funeral watched by more than two billion viewers worldwide.

'The People's Princess' had developed an extraordinary ability to touch people, and did much to destigmatise AIDS and leprosy, and raise awareness of the importance of post-conflict mine clearance. 'Her overall effect on charity', said Stephen Lee, director of the UK Institute of Charity Fundraising Managers, 'is probably more significant than any other person's in the twentieth century.'

Diana's death prompted an unprecedented outpouring of public grief, becoming a pivotal moment in the demise of the British stiff upper lip.

Edith Cavell Carrara marble on Cornish granite monument, 1920

By George Frampton

St Martin's Place, WC2N 4HA (opposite the National Portrait Gallery, at the bottom of St Martin's Lane)

This massive memorial, with a dignified, strait-laced Edith Cavell standing pure in white marble, is a monument not only to a heroic woman, but also to the power of wartime propaganda.

The oldest daughter of a Norfolk clergyman, Edith Cavell (1865–1915) worked as a governess, including

in Belgium, before training to be a nurse and serving in hospitals across London. In 1907 she was asked to become matron of the first Belgian nursing school, and had a significant impact on the development of modern nursing in the country. When Germany occupied Belgium in 1914, Cavell remained in Brussels treating wounded soldiers from both sides.

However, she was also secretly helping British and French soldiers, and willing military-age Belgians, to escape to the neutral Netherlands and (re)join the Allied forces. She sheltered at least 200 young men before being arrested. She neither denied her activities nor claimed not to know the consequences, so the Germans legitimately applied their law against 'War Treason' (aiding the enemy). There was little the Allies could do – though American diplomats tried – to prevent her execution by firing squad on 12 October 1915.

What the Allies could do was make propaganda use of her death, painting a picture of German depravity that stooped to the heartless murder of a caring British woman. The story of the 'martyr nurse' spread far and fast.

The Lord Mayor of London, the Bishop of

London, the Chairman of the London County Council and the aristocratic owner of the *Daily Telegraph* got together and, though Cavell's sister was against a monument, quickly commissioned this memorial. The sculptor George Frampton (best known for Peter Pan in Kensington Gardens) patriotically declined payment.

At the end of the war, Cavell's remains were among just three repatriated (including the Unknown Soldier's), and she became the first female commoner to receive a state funeral in Westminster Abbey. She was reburied at Norwich Cathedral, and is recognised by the Anglican church with a commemoration day on 12 October.

There are memorials to Cavell from Norwich to Inverness, Belgium to Australia. Nursing facilities, schools, even a bridge and a mountain are named after her – as, less predictably, was the famous French singer Edith Piaf.

Female Education

1. Christ's Hospital Memorial, Christchurch Greyfriars Garden, King Edward St, EC1A 7BA. Bronze, 2017. By Andrew F. Brown.

2. Bluecoat girl (and boy) – at multiple sites of former 'Bluecoat' charity schools, painted stone (or Coade stone). Seventeenth and eighteenth century.

• St John of Wapping (next to the church, now private housing), 6–8 Scandrett St, E1W 2UP. 1760, 'by subscription' (school founded 1695).

• Raine's House (now a 'community hub'), Raine St, E1W 3AQ. 1983 fibreglass casts (repainted 2021) of 1719 originals (these moved with the school in 1880s to Bethnal Green, where they are kept inside).

• Wren House/Old St Andrew's School (Hatton Chapel), Hatton Garden, EC1N 8EL (a school until Second World War, post-war rebuild as offices). 1721 (the girl and boy statues survived the war by being evacuated like real children).

• St Andrew's Church Holborn, 5 St Andrew St, EC4A 3AF. School founded 1696, moved to Hatton Garden 1721, where two pairs of children erected. After Second World War one pair was brought here.

• St Botolph-without-Bishopsgate Church Hall, EC2M 3TL. In a deeply historic City churchyard, two Coade stone Charity Children adorned the façade of the 1861 church hall that used to be a school. They were painted annually by pupils, but have now been moved inside for security, and replaced by unpainted modern copies.

3. Grey Coat girl (and boy), Grey Coat Hospital School, Greycoat Place, SW1P 2DY

A young woman and a young man lead a column of girls and boys of decreasing age and increasing modernity confidently into the future on the Christ's Hospital Memorial. Commemorating 350 years of the school in the City of London, it stands by the Second World War ruin of a Wren church (once used by the school), which

replaced a pre-Reformation monastery in the grounds of which the school opened in 1552.

Founded by Edward VI, the 'Hospital' – then a broader term for a hospitable place of refuge – was created for the care and education of poor boys and girls. Yes, in the sixteenth century King Edward saw fit to include girls.

Although boys and girls were generally not taught together, or the same things (boys receiving more literacy and numeracy), the school remained co-ed for all but the twentieth century(!). The first register in 1563 named 396 children, 132 of them girls. The proportion fell in later years, but the school was mixed until 1902, when the boys moved to Horsham (West Sussex), the girls to Hertfordshire. They were not reunited (at Horsham) until 1985, but today half of the 900 pupils are girls.

The school's charitable character continues too. More than two-thirds of pupils pay no or reduced fees. All receive free school uniform – and this is still the distinctive Tudor attire seen on the statue. What you can't see here is the colour: the coats are blue, the knee-length socks (beneath the coat) yellow.

Blue coats became a signifier of charity education, and little figures of girls and boys in blue are dotted across London on facades of former schools, often associated with religious buildings. These slightly later schools clothed girls in dresses and taught them mostly practical skills to ready them for domestic service, while boys were prepared for a trade. Although the little statues span decades, they are quite alike, the girl holding an open book or paper, the boy a closed book – although like the schools they also have their own character.

The Grey Coat Hospital girl and boy are similar too, although dressed (unsurprisingly) in grey. The school, now a Church of England girls' comprehensive, was founded in 1698 when the area was rife with poverty and crime. Eight concerned parishioners of St Margaret's Westminster (next to the abbey) aimed to educate poor children to be 'loyal citizens, useful workers and solid Christians'. The first intake was 11 boys, but by 1701 the school had bought a disused Elizabethan workhouse on its present site and included girls. In 1706 Queen Anne gave the school a

royal charter – and soon sent along two orphan girls. In 1713 she provided the pupils with prime seats at her lavish procession to the St Paul's thanksgiving service for the Treaty of Utrecht, as part of which her own statue was unveiled (p. 152). After a period of dire mismanagement, in 1874 the school became exclusively for girls.

Eleanor of Castile

Statues in Portland stone, monument red sandstone, 1865, after an original of 1291—4

Eight Queen Eleanors look out from this memorial, and she can be seen from all sides – exactly the visibility her husband King Edward I intended when he built 'Eleanor Crosses' across England. They stood at 12 overnight resting places of her body between Harby, Nottinghamshire, where she died, and Westminster Abbey, where she is buried – and since around 1830 also commemorated with a wavy-haired stone likeness on the exterior of the north nave.

The last and most elaborate cross was constructed at the nearby hamlet of Charing – quickly renamed Charing Cross. What we see today is a Victorian reconstruction of the thirteenth-century original, created when the station opened. It is based on surviving crosses at Geddington and Hardingstone (both in Northamptonshire) and Waltham Cross (Hertfordshire), as well as images of the Charing original.

This stood at the top of Whitehall on the spot now occupied by the equestrian statue of King Charles I (1630–3, re-erected here 1675) – London's oldest public statue of a man. Here Eleanor's Cross became the capital's official centre, from which mileages to London were (and are) measured.

In the civil war that saw Charles beheaded, however, many of the queen's crosses were destroyed. The Puritans objected to the monarchical and religious symbolism (ideological issues with statues aren't new); on the Charing cross today we see four Eleanors holding royal orb and sceptre and four carrying religious attributes. The original cross was removed by order of Parliament in 1647.

Eleanor (c. 1241–90) was the daughter of Ferdinand III of Castile and Jeanne of Ponthieu – hence Spanish and French coats of arms on the monument along with English. She was married to Prince Edward when she

was 12, and he 15.

Fortunately, they got on very well. Rarely apart, she accompanied him on military campaigns and their 16 children (six survived her) were born along the way, including one on crusade, and the future King Edward II while conquering Wales. Encouraged by Edward, Eleanor bought land (sometimes by questionable means) to give her financial security in the event of his demise, but in the end it was she who died first, leaving Edward to mourn through his Eleanor crosses.

A 1979 mural by David Gentleman on the Northern Line platforms of Charing Cross underground station narrates the creation of the original Charing cross from quarrying the stone to lifting Eleanor's statues into place.

Emmeline Pankhurst

Bronze, 1930, with memorial relief to Christabel Pankhurst added 1958–9

By Arthur George Walker RA (1861–1939), who had already made Florence Nightingale (p. 56) and Louisa Aldrich-Blake (p. 104)

Victoria Tower Gardens, Westminster, SW1A 0AA

The campaign for this monument began two weeks after the Suffragette leader's death in 1928. 'Men commemorate their heroes and liberators by erecting statues,' her followers noted; 'shall not women claim equal honour for her [*sic*] who led them to Victory.' They had quite a fight to make it happen, but they were used to that.

Emmeline Pankhurst (1858–1928) stands elegant in fur-trimmed coat, arms open as if addressing an audience. She looks an unlikely militant, but her organisation's campaigns included assaulting policemen, arson and bombings. This militancy led to a rift with non-violent campaigners and her two younger daughters, as well as clashes with police (who could also be violent), prison sentences, hunger strikes and painful force-feeding. Both the morality and the effectiveness of Pankhurst's methods are still debated.

This statue was nonetheless unveiled in 1930, almost nine decades before that to peaceful Suffragist Millicent Fawcett (p. 134). Newly ex-Prime Minister Stanley Baldwin did the honours, and music was provided by the band of the Metropolitan Police! In 1958 the statue was moved across the gardens and the memorial to Emmeline's recently-deceased co-militant daughter, Christabel Pankhurst (1880–1958), was added.

Emmeline was born into a comfortably-off, politically engaged Manchester family, and met her husband, activist

Mrs Pankhurst in Trafalgar Square, 13 October 1908, before rushing Parliament.

lawyer Richard Pankhurst, at a public meeting. Horrified by the privation endured by poor women in Manchester, she tried to join the local branch of the Independent Labour Party but was initially refused because she was a woman. By 1903 she had lost patience with polite politicking and founded the all-female Women's Social and Political Union (WSPU), the 'suffrage army', to campaign single-mindedly for the vote with 'deeds, not words'.

During World War I (1914–18), the Pankhursts suspended their suffrage activism and encouraged men to fight and women to work for the war effort. In 1918 voting was extended to all men over 21 and most women over 30. The discrepancy was not simply sexist, but intended to equalise male and female voter numbers after so many young men had died in the war.

Emmeline turned the WSPU into the Women's Party and fought for equality in public life. Increasingly right-leaning and fearing Bolshevism, in 1927 she became a Conservative parliamentary candidate. Illness intervened, however, and in 1928 she died just weeks before the granting of universal suffrage over 21.

Florence Nightingale Bronze, 1915

By Arthur George Walker, who also made Louisa Aldrich-Blake (p. 104) and Emmeline Pankhurst (p. 64)

Part of a larger Crimean War Memorial, Waterloo Place, St James's, SW1Y 5NP

Waterloo Place is an outdoor museum of memorial statues. All are male, except for allegorical figures of Britannia, Honour/Victory, a golden Athena, and one real woman – Florence Nightingale.

Commissioned straight after the famous nurse's death in 1910, the 'Lady with the Lamp' statue was unveiled without ceremony midway through World War I, when the 1860s Crimean War Memorial here was reconfigured to accommodate it. Reported at the time, and often since, to be London's first monument to a named non-royal female, it wasn't: the marble figure of actress Sarah Siddons (p. 176) was erected in 1897 and Margaret MacDonald's memorial (p. 106) in 1914.

Florence Nightingale (1820–1910) was named for the Italian city of her birth, where her wealthy, well-connected, liberal parents were on the Grand Tour. Educated more than was usual for a Victorian girl, she was clever, particularly at maths, and religious. Declaring herself called by God, she trained, against her family's wishes, to nurse.

Nightingale ran an institution for sick gentlewomen in Harley Street until, in 1854, her friend Sidney Herbert, the War Secretary, asked her to lead a group of 38 nurses to the military hospital at Scutari in Turkey, where soldiers from the Crimean War were dying at an alarming rate. Nightingale's statue is paired with one of a thoughtful-looking Herbert atop an identical plinth, with bronze reliefs of their overlapping roles.

In Scutari Nightingale improved hygiene, diet, medical supplies and humanity at the hospital, and is said to have reduced the mortality rate from 42 per cent to 2 per cent. She carefully recorded her activities, adduced statistics and made pioneering use of infographics to communicate her data – skills

recognised in 1859 when she was elected the first female member of the Royal Statistical Society.

Her methodical approach allowed her improvements to be replicated, and she had a major impact on public as well as military health from England to India. In 1860 she founded the world's first secular nursing school at St Thomas' Hospital (now the Florence Nightingale Faculty of Nursing), though it is another Crimean War nurse, Mary Seacole, who is most visibly memorialised there (p. 126).

Even before Crimea, Nightingale was depressive. Her work took its toll, and in 1856 Queen Victoria (p. 164) described her as 'tall and slight . . . must have been pretty but now . . . very thin and careworn'. She was largely housebound for decades before her death, aged 90, at home in South Street, Mayfair, just a mile from where her effigy stands today.

Girl with a Dolphin Bronze (with a waterspout), 1973

By David Wynne (1926–2014)

St Katharine's Way, by Tower Bridge Quay (north bank of Thames, east side of Tower Bridge), E1W 1YL

On the bank of the River Thames by Tower Bridge stands a statue of a woman (clearly not a girl) diving down to touch a dolphin. The sculpture flows in one delightful sweep from the tips of her human toes to the fluke of the dolphin's tail, on which the entire structure stands.

It's an engineering as well as an artistic feat, and – with or without the water jet that streams over the connected bodies – it has an astonishingly aquatic feel. The dolphin boasts a beguiling cetacean half-smile, while the woman's hair cascades behind her, while her legs hang loose 'in the water'.

The sculptor, David Wynne (better known for his dynamic *Boy with a Dolphin* in Chelsea), went to Cambridge to read zoology. But he was such an inattentive student that the master of his college, so the story goes, wrote to him, 'You will be more use in the world as a sculptor than as a zoologist, you are therefore excused all lectures' (those were different times).

Wynne nonetheless assiduously studied the animals he depicted in his sculptures – and was condemned by the 'progressive' art world for being unfashionably figurative in the age of abstraction. His humans too he sculpted from life, and this girl/woman is no imagined classical nude. Indeed, in 2023, 50 years after the statue was unveiled, the unlikely model revealed her identity.

This naked diver is British tennis star Virginia Wade. She was 28 at the time, already a sporting household name and double grand slam winner, soon to be Wimbledon champion (1977). Wynne, a

Virginia Wade victorious in the Women's Singles at Wimbledon in 1977.

tennis fan and amateur player, met Wade in the early 1970s, knocked a few balls with her, made a couple of statues of her, and then asked if she would pose for *Girl with a Dolphin*. She hesitated – owing to the nudity – but agreed. 'He was very professional,' she has since said. They agreed to use her body but not her face, and to keep her role a secret.

Even in 2023 the revelation surprised many. Wade's reputation has always been rather proper, while the statue is the epitome of physical freedom. 'It gives me a warm feeling that I was involved,' Wade told the *Sunday Times*. She likes Wynne's sculptures that named her, 'but they're just me . . . *Girl with a Dolphin* is . . . gorgeous.'

Women, women . . .

What to do with a bunch of wonderful, indefinable women?

If only we knew the answer in life. At least here we can randomly include them, admitting to no categorisation other than that they are female and neither real individuals nor conventional classical personifications. Ranging from playful nudes to arty abstractions, nearly 'normal people' (p. 76) to fictional/poetic personifications, these are the ones not mentioned elsewhere that we didn't want to leave out . . .

Gravity- and genre-defying, *Leaning Woman* is an intriguing combination of classical and modern, active and calm. She stands with her back to a little public garden facing the roaring A4. This is not an accident. She was given to the local community by the London County Council in (rather inadequate) compensation for the six-lane highway cutting through their neighbourhood. Her oversized, draped lower body anchors her, while her naked torso reaches along the nearside lane, her arms folded as if on the sill of an invisible window through which she is watching the cars rush by. The sculptor (a Czech refugee from Nazi Germany) apparently had the model, East German émigré Jutta Cardew, pose leaning on an upturned broom. The sculpture's reception was initially mixed — a local councillor described it as a 'modern monstrosity' — but *Leaning*

Woman gained favour, and in 2024 her crumbling concrete body was fully restored.

This vibrant fantasy woman strides confidently forward, a little ditzy, one hand clutching her designer handbag, the other determinedly clenched. Sadly now rather hidden next to the bins, she stands in memory of a real, 'lively, ambitious' woman, Joan Roberts, who worked at the Royal Free and died of cancer in her forties. She left money for a statue, and her former colleagues chose this jubilant character from the 1964 Manfred Mann hit 'Do Wah Diddy' (yes, the statue gained an 'o'). They liked its upbeat feel, and especially the handbag — Roberts had her ashes interred in a Gucci bag.

Ships' figureheads were traditionally female, and so is this dynamic, richly textured statue full of striking silhouettes. The artist (also female) says the figure refers to the London docks' original role at the centre of seafaring trade, while its use of recycled materials reflects the renovation and repurposing of the docklands for contemporary London.

 Connaught Bridge Roundabout, Connaught Rd (at the western end of London City Airport's runway), E16 2FA. Bronze painted silver, 2012. By Nasser Azam (b. 1963).

This dynamic naked 12-metre female figure — the tallest bronze statue in Britain — reaches for the sky, glistening silver like the planes that fly low over her head in and out of City Airport.

Installed in the year of the London Olympics, she is curved like a gymnast about to spring, to take off along with the planes. The sculptor, who grew up nearby, said he intended it to be 'uplifting, inspiring and easily recognisable' — not as Athena, perhaps, but as itself. And it is.

Crouching Figure Outside the Connaught Hotel, Carlos Place, Mayfair, W1K 2AL. Bronze, 1973, here since 1987. By Emilio Greco.

Curled up, almost contorted, and sometimes titled *Nymph*, this smooth-skinned nude perches on a rock or knoll. Her hair

echoes the texture of the ground, into which her feet and one hand meld as though she has emerged from it. Given to the City of Westminster by the president of Italy, she was paid for by Italian banks in London.

Goatherd's Daughter/The Shepherdess St John's Lodge Gardens, Regent's Park, NW1 4NX. Bronze, won the Royal British Society of Sculptors Silver Medal in 1929, first unveiled 1932, installed here 1994. By Charles Leonard Hartwell (1873–1951).

This melancholy, semi-naked young woman carries a kid goat under her arm and an inscription: 'To all the protectors of the defenceless' — and she looks pretty defenceless herself. She was installed here by the National Council for Animal Welfare in memory of Harold and Gertrude Baillie Weaver, campaigners against vivisection and for vegetarianism and women's suffrage. Gertrude (1855–1926) was a writer, publishing works of fact, fiction and poetry (mostly under her first married name, Gertrude Colmore) in support of the rights of women and animals.

Born in Berlin, sculptor Gerda Rubinstein grew up in Amsterdam. Her Jewish father was murdered by the Nazis, but her Christian mother and the children survived. In 1958 Rubinstein came to London, and stayed, teaching in Catford for many years. Her public sculptures, almost all of people, are, as she said herself, 'self-explanatory', and tend to inspire affection.

This is no exception, a lovely, gentle piece depicting a young woman sitting on the grass in summer clothes, feet bare, half smiling, happily thinking to herself. 'I have come to realise,' Rubinstein once said, 'that the sense of freedom and hope that I experienced as a teenager in Holland, after five years of occupation in World War Two, has really never left me, and that it still colours my work.'

The artist asks us to look 'without preconceptions of form or meaning', so the gender of most of these semi-abstract sculptures is undefined, but eight out of nine of them appear to include a female figure.

Judy (with Punch) and *Motherfigure* (an uncomfortable image involving pregnancy) do so unambiguously. In *Pygmalion*, two figures cling together. He is the legendary sculptor in Ovid's *Metamorphoses* who, 'detesting beyond measure the faults which nature has given to women', commits his life to art, only to make a statue of a woman so perfect he falls in love with it. Rather disturbingly (and several of these statues are disturbing), the story continues that the goddess Aphrodite brings the statue to life and they live happily ever after. Other sculptures on the trail have loaded names like *Fall* (referring to the creation myth of woman as misleader of men?) and *Exodus*.

OK, she's too young to be a woman, but this lively, laughing, skipping girl, modelled on the artist's daughter, makes me smile, and she's quite the local landmark. As an adult the real Kate reflected on how flattered she was to have the statue named after her, adding, 'It's always been funny to think of all the people in Harrow who over the years have said, "Let's go and meet under *Katie*"!'

Hygeia Hygeia House, 66–68 College Road, Harrow, HA1 1BE. By Rudy Weller, 1991.

Opposite Harrow-on-the-Hill Station, this golden, semi-naked, 1990s Greek goddess dances out of the façade of an office block. Hygeia was the Ancient Greek goddess of health and cleanliness (the derivation of the word hygiene), and here she is displayed in vibrant 'tits' glory (see p. 100). 'My composition shows her leaping into the unknown,' says the sculptor Rudy Weller, 'the confidence of youth with trusting outstretched arms (see also Three Graces p. 186). My aim was to create a positive image of hope for the future.'

London Pride Queen's Walk, South Bank, SE1 9PX. Designed 1951, cast in bronze and installed here 1987. By Frank Dobson (1886–1963).

Two women sit naked outside the National Theatre. The statue does not seem intended to titillate; the women are just doing their own thing, chatting perhaps. It was commissioned for the 1951 Great Exhibition, a celebration of British achievement and optimism after World War II which took place on this bank of the Thames. The artist intended the bowl to be planted with the flower London Pride (*saxifraga urbium*, after which the beer is also named), which grew in crevices across bomb-damaged London. It was popularised as a symbol of plucky survival by a Noel Coward song of the same name written during the Blitz, singing of a flower that was free and meant 'our own dear town'. Removed after the exhibition, the sculpture was donated by the artist's wife and placed here in 1987, by which time the South Bank had become one of London's most important centres of performance and exhibition.

Three Fates LSE Campus, outside Pethick Lawrence House, WC2A 2AZ. Bronze figures on painted steel poles, 2003. By Morton Katz.

The Three Fates or Moirai were Greek mythological sisters, usually said to be daughters of Zeus, whose role was to weave our destinies and control our deaths. Though they are customarily depicted as idealised young women, these three, atop colourful poles on a campus walkway, are thoroughly human. Rough-skinned, variously and realistically shaped, they are naked and posed, but not titillating. One looks melancholy (perhaps Atropos, who traditionally cut the thread of life); the other two seem more confident and in charge of their own (and maybe our) destinies.

Pastorale 1–2 Parkleys Parade, Ham, TW10 5LR (on a patch of grass behind a hedge next to the shops at the entrance to the estate). Bronze, 1956. By Keith Godwin (1916–91).

Unveiled by the already well-known champion of modern architecture Sir Hugh Casson at the entrance to the then-new, ultra-modern, award-winning Parkleys estate (now listed), this a-little-larger-than-life statue was initially controversial. The criticism didn't last; the statue did. Representing home-making, this is a surprisingly touching, stylised depiction of a naked woman communing with a bird at its chick-filled nest, the woman and the mother bird looking directly into each other's eyes.

Golders Hill Girl Bronze, 1991

By Patricia Finch (1921–2001)
Golders Hill Park, NW3 7HE
See also: *Mother and Child* by Patricia Finch, p. 146

She sits in shorts and T-shirt, bare legs outstretched, enjoying a sunny day in the park. But *Golders Hill Girl* isn't really about the girl; it's a tribute to the park itself. In summer, kids plonk themselves on her lap or stroke her hair, polishing it golden, while adults pose beside her. And on cold, grey, winter days she sits there still, amid rouged berries and fire-red stems, scantily clad, flip-flops off, a welcome reminder that summer will return.

Modelled (at least facially) on Helen Scott Lidgett (1948–2012), an arts PR and culture adviser to Prime Minister Gordon Brown, it was made by her mother, sculptor Patricia Finch, a lifelong local resident. 'My mother was born and died in the same bed in Golders Green,' says Finch's younger daughter, the musician and ex-Radio 3 presenter Lucie Skeaping. 'She was wheeled in her pram around this park from birth – so was my sister, so was I.'

'Much later in life, my father suggested she make a sculpture for the park that meant so much to her. My mother rarely did full bodies – most of her work was portrait heads – but she made the girl. I said – I take credit for this – "She needs sandals." My mother bronzed her own size 7's and we used to debate whether the girl had big enough feet to wear them.'

In 2003 one of them was stolen. 'Shoe done it?' yelled a local headline. Park authorities tracked down Skeaping, who bought a similar pair from Camden Market and gave them to the original foundry. *Golders Hill Girl* gained perhaps the most expensive pair of flip-flops in town: price tag £1,000.

'I don't think of it as my sister,' continues Skeaping – 'we never got on. In fact, I don't remember being told it was Helen until much later. Maybe it looked like her in retrospect, or perhaps my mother was being diplomatic. If she'd told me it was Helen I'd certainly have said, "Why don't you do me?"!'

'I don't think it's my mother's best work, but it is real community art. Kids love it. It's a great big doll, really. I used to meet my parents here sometimes, and I remember watching a little girl pick a flower and take it to the statue, holding it under her nose to smell.'

Patricia Finch sculpting during the 1950s with her nine-year-old daughter Helen, later the model for *Golders Hill Girl*.

Normal People — statues of us and among us

In Exchange Square, EC2A 2EH, a gaggle of people, three of them women, hurry, collars turned up against the weather, eyes blank, towards Liverpool Street Station. *Rush Hour* (1983–7), by George Segal (1924–2000), was one of the first of what might be called London's 'normal people' statues. New York sculptor Segal had been making this sort of art in America for a while. He pioneered the use of plaster bandages as a way of creating moulds from live

models – the technique used for another early 'normal people' installation in London, *Platforms Piece* at Brixton Station (1986, p. 86).

More 'normal people' statues followed. Among the women, *Golders Hill Girl* (p. 74) sits, life-size, sunning herself in the park, while in *Relationships* (1997, corner of Park Royal Rd and Acton Lane, NW10 7JJ) sculptor Sue Groom (b. 1941) places the bronze figure of a woman on the end of a bench opposite a superstore. The woman is rummaging in her basket, perhaps for a snack for the little girl who stands beside her (and maybe also the expectant-looking dog). We are clearly invited to sit down beside them. This is public art both for and about us.

Outside a café in Canary Wharf (George St, Wood Wharf, E14 5GX), *Standing Woman* (by Sean Henry, 2020) stands life-like, though more than life size, looking at *Standing Man* (2019). Painted in natural colours, she looks mildly irritated. Is he late? Or, since he is the one by the café door, is she? Either way, they are ourselves writ large.

Teulu ('Family' in Welsh, 1985) by Robert Thomas (1926–99) sees a bronze mother, father and two kids take up a whole bench in the middle of Ealing Broadway shopping centre, while just off the

King's Road (Duke of York Square, SW3 4LY), a boy leapfrogs a bollard and a girl sits nearby with a book looking concerned. These *Two Pupils* (by Allister Bowtell, 2002) are natural, life-size and right among us, but they are ghosts (note the historic dress) commemorating the bicentenary of the nearby Royal Military Asylum boarding school for children of deceased soldiers.

Roller Skater (2010, corner of Moreton Rd and Vauxhall Bridge Rd, SW1V 2PX) by Andrew Wallace (b. 1949) is a little larger than life and more geometric – and roller skating on a bench with strapless skates would not go so well in the real world. But she is just there doing her thing – and much loved by the girls' skating group based 100m away. The artist said he wanted the girl to convey independence and 'attitude' – and she does.

This trend for figures that are not raised above us, but merge with us and invite direct interaction, has rubbed off on statues of the famous. The slight figure of Amy Winehouse hangs out in Camden Market (p. 24), while Virginia Woolf sits on a bench at Richmond Riverside (p. 202). The Salter family (p. 14) stand on the bank of the Thames, while Twiggy (p. 192), though a little abstracted, poses on the pavement. This installation even includes a bronze passer-by stopping, like us, to look.

It's a far cry from heroes on high pedestals, and generally regarded as a positive development. It's interesting to see where the statues are polished by the public's touch (note Amy's shoulder), though it does mean the statues have to be quite robust.

Ladies of the Bank

Architect Herbert Baker, sculptor Charles Wheeler (1892–1974)

The Old Lady of Threadneedle Street, Portland stone, 1930.

Ariel, gilded bronze, 1936.

Bank of England, Threadneedle Street, EC2R 8AH

The 'Old Lady' – more correctly Britannia (see also p. 42) – sits on a globe, high in the pediment of the Bank of England, coins cascading at her side, holding a model of the bank. She's been here since 1930, but her status goes back much further.

The bank itself became known as 'the Old Lady of Threadneedle Street' after a 1797 cartoon by arch political cartoonist James Gillray. Published when the government was trying to get its hands on the bank's gold reserves, the image shows the Prime Minister, William Pitt the Younger, trying to kiss an old lady clothed in banknotes and seated firmly on a closed gold chest, while his hands wander to her coin-filled pockets.

The nickname soon rubbed off on the elegant, mid-eighteenth-century Britannia that then sat with a cornucopia of coins in the bank's pediment. In the 1930s the building was almost completely reconstructed, and this 'Old Lady of the Bank' was replaced with the more modern one we see today.

Not everyone was impressed. One stockholder declared her a monstrosity, and as a personification of the bank she was ripe for ribaldry. 'Miss Threadneedle Street is wearing a permanent wave and not a great deal else,' declared an *Evening News* editorial in October 1930:

> *The lady . . . appears to be in the act of removing her bathrobe . . . For the rest, [she] has a hard eye, a disagreeable mouth and . . . [her] right hand – presumably the one that wields the bullion scoop – is terrific. You can feel that once your money got into that heroic grip nothing would pry it loose again – not even you.*

The Bank's governor defended Charles Wheeler's sculpture, assuring critics that they would soon come to admire it. And they did. Indeed, Wheeler was twice asked to reprise the image: for the bank's 1940 Southampton branch (on the High Street, now student accommodation), and on a City extension now demolished.

left: Political Ravishment or The Old Lady of Threadneedle Street in Danger by James Gillray, 1797

The bank has other Wheeler women: two caryatids – for once less naked than their starkers male counterparts – and, on the Lothbury facade at the back, four lightly-draped 'Lothbury Ladies'. But the most famous other lady of the bank is undoubtedly its light-footed, dome-topping, golden Ariel. Yes, that's right, a female Ariel.

Magical Prospero's male servant spirit in Shakespeare's *The Tempest*, who could 'put a girdle round the earth in forty minutes', was seen as an ideal emblem for this globally important imperial bank. But 'not to miss an excuse for another artfully draped female figure', says the Bank museum's curator Jenni Adam, this Ariel is a woman. The long-serving governor of the bank, Montagu Norman, apparently couldn't get his head round the gender shift, and insisted on calling this visibly female figure 'he'. Fair enough perhaps if, as Philip Ward-Jackson suggests in

The original 'Old Lady' Britannia from the Bank of England façade, probably by Robert Taylor between 1734 and 1788.

The current Old Lady from 1930.

his *Public Sculpture of the City of London*, images inside the bank and contemporary comments show that Norman was considered this Ariel's Prospero.

Two of the four 'Lothbury Ladies', one with a coin hoard, the other with a child representing the future of the rebuilt bank. Charles Wheeler, 1932–4.

Ariel, 1936. Referred to by the Bank's architect as 'the Arielesque Lady'.

Joan Littlewood The Mother of Modern Theatre, bronze, 2015

By Philip Jackson

In front of the Theatre Royal, Stratford, Theatre Square, E15 1BN

In flat cap and donkey jacket, Joan Littlewood (1914–2002) sits on a pile of brick rubble outside her theatre, smiling to herself. The statue is based on a 1970s photo taken when this neighbourhood was largely demolished and the theatre only just survived. The rubble also evokes its semi-dereliction in 1953 when Littlewood and her Theatre Workshop moved in – literally. With no money, they slept in the dressing rooms and did the renovation themselves.

Joan Littlewood talks to the actress Barbara Windsor in 1964 before a tour of *Oh! What a Lovely War!*

Born in Stockwell, the illegitimate daughter of a teenage maid, Littlewood spent her own teens as a grammar school scholarship girl 'seeing everything' in London's theatres. Another scholarship took her to leading drama school, RADA, but she found it narrow and snobby and left. Moving to Manchester, she married the singer-songwriter Ewan MacColl (later father of Kirsty), with whom she did political theatre and worked for the BBC – until they were blacklisted as Communists.

In 1945 they started their own experimental theatre company, travelling the country by lorry to bring theatre to the working classes. Theoretically the company had no hierarchy, but nobody doubted who was in charge. 'I don't give a damn if I sound like a paranoid egomaniac,' Littlewood told a radio interviewer – 'I am.' The flat cap was apparently a sign of mood: peak up, you're OK; pulled down, look out! But the company also enjoyed intense creativity, camaraderie and laughter. Those who could cope would have followed her to the ends of the earth – and more or less did.

After eight years' solid touring (with no fixed pay), the company settled in Stratford, creating a 'people's theatre' for and with the underprivileged local community. Combining cutting-edge Continental intellectual ideas (she was a big fan of Bertolt Brecht) with popular British theatrical traditions, Littlewood's ground-breaking productions revolutionised British theatre, most famously in 1963's satirical anti-war musical *Oh! What a Lovely War!* She was a key influence on younger directors like Peter Hall and Trevor Nunn.

In 1975, devastated by the death of her theatre manager and by now life partner Gerry Raffles, Littlewood left the theatre, eventually settling in France in an unlikely relationship with the writer and millionaire wine-maker Baron Philippe de Rothschild. But she never lost her iconoclasm. When in 1994 Richard Eyre wrote to her asking to stage *Oh! What a Lovely War!* at the National Theatre she suggested he blow the place up.

Joy Battick Bronze: *Platforms Piece*, 1986; *Joy II*, 2023

By Kevin Atherton (b. 1950)

Brixton Station (National Rail, above Brixton Market), SW9 8JB (there is free access to the platforms)

See also: interview with Joy Battick, p. 88

A young black woman with a determined, don't-mess-with-me look stands hands-on-hips in Umbro jacket, trainers and hoop earrings, on platform 1 of Brixton railway station. On platform 2 opposite, an older woman in a polo neck and beret echoes the younger woman's stance, but she looks more comfortable and smiles warmly across the rails. Both are Joy Battick, immortalised in bronze 37 years apart.

The earlier figure, unveiled in 1986, is the first public statue of an individual woman of colour in London. It was created as part of *Platforms Piece*, a sculpture of three bronze Brixton locals 'waiting for their trains'.

The other two are Peter Lloyd (probably London's first public statue of an individual black man) and Karin Heistermann, a young white woman approached in 1985 by the sculptor, Kevin Atherton, before she boarded her train to work.

'It was a bit awkward,' he tells me. 'I had to ask a female member of station staff to help. It would have been a bit threatening as a random man to say, "I've been watching you for a week and I'd like to make a sculpture of you . . . It involves being in a swimsuit covered in baby oil, wet plaster bandages and Vaseline"!'

Heistermann said yes. 'Then I needed two black people.' Atherton wasn't conscious of making public art history: 'It was just a no-brainer to reflect Brixton.' But the 1985 Brixton riots intervened, and when Atherton, a white Manxman, approached a young black man at the station, 'he looked straight through me. I don't blame him.' So Atherton sought help locally, and Lloyd and Battick were recruited from the neighbouring Brixton Recreation Centre. All three Brixtonians had their bodies cast on site in a repurposed ticket office, and Sir Hugh Casson (then just ex-president of the Royal Academy) unveiled them.

In 2016 Atherton discovered that his Heistermann

Joy II

statue had been removed due to damage and Joy was almost invisible behind a new safety fence. He re-engaged. The statues were sent for restoration, and Atherton asked to add *Joy II*. 'Contacting her was quite emotional. I hadn't seen her in thirty-six years, and she had recently survived cancer' (see interview, p. 88).

This time her body was digitally scanned, and in 2023 all four statues were (re)unveiled with Battick and Heistermann attending. *Joy II* has beside her the same bag as *Joy I*, but she looks back at her younger self across a lifetime.

Joy I

An Interview with Joy Battick

Model for the first public statue of a woman of colour in London in 1986, and a second 36 years later (see p. 86)

'In 1986 we were just coming out of the Brixton riots. When I look at my first statue now, I can see how serious it was for me as a young person of colour. It was a harsh, tense time, and it shows. I was fit and healthy, but I wasn't happy.

'The leisure centre where I worked was a bit of a political football after the riots; it got a lot of attention. And then suddenly there was Kevin asking for two people to do a sculpture. There wasn't much talk. I did it because it got me out of being poolside at 7.30 a.m.!

'I had no idea we were making history. I didn't know it was London's first statue of a woman of colour

until it was listed [by Historic England] in 2016. I was told I'd be 'immortalised', but that meant nothing to me then. It does now – and it feels great.

'My father came over on the *Windrush*, my mother followed five years later. He got whatever work he could, but they were exploited. I think the Windrush Memorial [p. 208] is fantastic. It doesn't make up for anything, and there needs to be much more done for the people, but the statue is brilliant, and seeing my parents understood in sculpture makes me go a bit goose-pimply.

'When Kevin contacted me to do the second statue, I was just finishing treatment for breast cancer. That had scared the living daylights out of me, and making

the statue was a real tonic – it makes me feel I'm still in the game.

'This time Kevin and I talked – and we still do. And I didn't have to have my nose and ears blocked and get covered in plaster (which was awful!). Instead I went to the Marvel studio for a 3D scan. It used 165 camera angles – like being on a modelling shoot for *Vogue*!

'The unveiling was super. Karin [Heistermann] came. Peter [Lloyd] didn't. In my new statue, I look so happy. There's been trauma, but I've settled into my life. The expressions on my statues tell everything.

'My children love them, and I'm really looking forward to introducing my granddaughter – who is one – to the statues. I live in Croydon now, but I come back to Brixton, especially for the market. When I do, I always pop up to see my good self standing on the platform. People wave at me. I don't usually wave back, of course. But if *I'm* there – I do!'

Justice Gilt bronze; other figures in Portland stone, 1905–6

By Frederick William Pomeroy (1856–1924).
Commissioned by the building's architect,
Edward William Mountford.

Old Bailey, EC4M 7EH

See also: Supreme Court (p. 178); Samuel Plimsoll
memorial (Laid Bare, p. 100); atop Foreign, Commonwealth
and Development Office (FCDO) façade with Queen
Victoria as Britannia (p. 42)

The golden Lady Justice atop the Old Bailey glows over
the streets of the City, a genuinely iconic symbol of
the Central Criminal Court of England and Wales.

The stern face of this 3.65m, classically-draped figure is not visible from the ground more than 60m below (unless with binoculars/zoom), but her spikey crown and the golden globe she stands

Law Society blind Justice, 113 Chancery Lane. By Charles Pibworth, 1902–4.

left: Blind Justice with accountants behind, Institute of Chartered Accountants, Moorgate Place, by William Hamo Thornycroft, 1892–3.

on are clear against the sky. So too are her judicial attributes: the upright sword of truth and the balanced scales of justice.

Justice is almost always personified as a woman, harking back to the Ancient Roman goddess Justicia. She was a bit of a latecomer to the Roman pantheon, introduced by Augustus (Octavian), first Emperor of Rome (27 BC–14 AD), but Justicia was in turn descended from Greek goddesses Themis and Dike and the Ancient Egyptian Maat, goddess of justice, truth, and harmony.

On the Old Bailey, Lady Justice has a backing group of five further female allegorical figures. Three top the main entrance: a suitably solid Angel of Record

The Old Bailey

flanked by muscular Fortitude and a now rather worn Truth (with mirror and snake, symbol of knowledge) – all unhelpfully shrouded in protective black netting. More visible and better preserved are two separate bare-breasted figures. Neither is named, but both fit pleasingly into the architecture. The figure on the left may be Truth, as she holds a sword and her other hand rests on a (legal?) book. The right-hand woman crouches with a book and quill pen.

It was noted when the public first saw this building that the Justice was not blindfold. Justice had recently been depicted as 'blind Justice' on several City buildings, including a topless figure at the Law Society on Chancery Lane, and two Justices among other virtues on Moorgate's Metropolitan Life Assurance Building (by William Silver Frith, who later made a quite different Justice for the Edward VII Jewish Memorial Drinking Fountain, p. 35). At the Institute

Blind Justice, Metropolitan Life Assurance Building,
13 Moorgate, EC2R 6AD. By William Silver Frith, 1890–3.

of Chartered Accountants, too, a blindfold Justice
dominated an elaborate and much-admired scheme of
architectural carving – and comprehensively eclipsed a
couple of stone accountants beavering away behind her.
Appropriate symbolism for a regulatory Institution.

Justice's blindfold was of course intended to
indicate her impartiality and immunity to extraneous
influences but, amusingly, the symbolism may
originally have been satirical, denoting quite the
opposite. The first known depiction of Justice
blindfold is a woodcut, the Fool Blinding Justice
(sometimes attributed to Albrecht Dürer), illustrating
a popular critical verse satire, *Das Narrenschiff* (*The
Ship of Fools*),
1495, by the
Swiss humanist
and theologian
Sebastian Brant.

So perhaps
it's a good thing
that the Old
Bailey's Justice
is not just eye-
catching but
clear-eyed.

Blind Justice on the
Supreme Court

A few more Lady Justices in London

Blindfold Justice in a sculptural group with female Prudence (see p. 148) and a winged child Liberality. Norwich Union Building (also by the entrance to Serjeants' Inn, then a legal location), 49–50 Fleet St, EC4A 2EA. Portland Stone, 1913. By Arthur Stanley Young.

Justice curled onto the corner of the 41m clock tower, bare-breasted, a single drape wrapped artfully around her lower body and head, hooding her eyes. Lambeth Town Hall (on the tower, with Science, Literature and Art), 1 Brixton Hill (corner of Acre Lane), SW2 1RW. Stone with metal sword and scales, 1908. By William Reid Dick.

Justice not blindfold, with sword. Left side of entrance arch to Middle Temple Lane from the Thames (at the heart of London's legal quarter). By William Calder Marshall, 1879.

Justice (not blindfold) stands with scales and downward-pointing sword. Bethnal Green Town Hall (now Town Hall Hotel), Patriot Square, E2 9NF. By Henry Poole, 1910.

Lady Henry Somerset Memorial Bronze, 1999, copy of stolen 1897 original

By George Edward Wade (1853–1933),
copy by Philomena Davidson Davis (b. 1949)

Victoria Embankment Gardens (Temple),
WC2R 2PH

A girl stands holding out a bowl, Oliver Twist-style. Water once flowed from the bowl, and the inscription on the granite base reads: 'I was thirsty and ye gave me drink.' Not alcoholic, presumably, since the statue is dedicated, 'From the children of the Loyal

Lady Henry Somerset distributes cabbages to children.

Temperance Legion in memory of the work done for the temperance cause by Lady Henry Somerset'. Lady Isabella Somerset (1851–1921), to give her the name she preferred, was not a typical pious exponent of alcoholic abstinence.

Daughter of the 3rd Earl Somers and his socialite wife, owners of estates in Herefordshire, Worcestershire, Reigate and London's Somers Town, Isabella married Lord Henry Somerset when she was 20. It was not a success. They produced one child, but Lord Henry was gay and wished to do as he pleased (then a criminal offence). The couple separated, and Lady Somerset broke with convention and fought for custody of her son. She won, but in the process revealed her husband's homosexuality, for which she was ostracised by 'polite' society.

This gave a high-born lady an unusual insight into the impact of being looked down upon and, particularly after a religious Damascene moment, she put this understanding to good use. Visiting the poor, she was appalled by the social destruction wreaked by alcohol, so she set up a farm village for alcoholic women, claiming a cure rate of about 70 per cent. She ran two homes to train workhouse women for domestic service, and was soon campaigning for contraception, declaring that sin started with an unwelcome child.

In 1890 Lady Somerset was elected President of the British Women's Temperance Association. An effective orator, she was soon using her platform, despite disapproval from other members, to campaign more broadly for women's welfare and for the vote. Her selflessness and success made her popular with the working class, and eventually restored her to 'society'.

This commemorative statue-cum-drinking fountain was erected when she was 45, the same year the first statue of a named non-royal woman was unveiled in London (p. 176). The children's statue dedicated to Lady Somerset stood for three-quarters of a century, until in 1971 it was sawn off at the feet and stolen. The plinth stood empty for 28 years until a replacement was made – incidentally by the first female president of the Royal British Society of Sculptors, Philomena Davidson Davis.

Lai Dai Han Mother and Child

Bronze, 2019, first unveiled at Church House but soon moved to its present location

Seeming to emerge organically from the ground, this touching statue of a tree-like mother and the child she protects was commissioned by Justice for Lai Dai Han, a campaign giving voice to victims of sexual and gender-based violence in conflicts, particularly the Lai Dai Han (meaning 'mixed blood' in Vietnamese). They are the thousands of children born to Vietnamese women as a result of rape, or relationship and abandonment, by South Korean soldiers fighting alongside the Americans in the Vietnam War.

The Lai Dai Han mothers and children not only have to cope with their traumatic origins but also, even 50 years on, face stigma, exclusion and poverty in Vietnam and denial of their existence by South Korea.

The mother in this sculpture looks desperately skyward, her tree-body entangled in a parasitic Strangler Fig tree (common in Vietnam). Rooted to the ground, she strains forward but cannot progress. Nonetheless, she gently cups the head of her child, who has separate roots and is both protected by her and provides a little support. With echoes of Rodin and Camille Claudel, and a touch of Giacometti, it's a work that, given a moment's quiet contemplation, has real emotional heft.

It was unveiled in 2019 by the 2018 Nobel Peace Prize winner Nadia Murad, herself a Yazidi victim of sexual violence at the hands of Islamic State, along with former foreign secretaries Jack Straw (Labour) and William Hague (Conservative). The sculpture was only meant to stay in St James's Gardens temporarily, but by the time the Covid hiatus was over, support for it remaining was such that it is now a permanent fixture.

The unveiling of the statue in 2019.

"

The sculptor, Rebecca Hawkins, is delighted it has found a peaceful, high-profile home. 'It's brilliant for the Lai Dai Han women and children,' she tells me. 'In Vietnam they are forbidden by law to even talk about their experiences, and they've been fighting diplomatically for an apology from South Korea for decades. A sculpture can't solve that, but they tell me that having a statue in a prestigious London location at least makes them feel heard and seen.'

Leopoldine (Leo) Avico

Commissioned to celebrate the twenty-first birthday of department store Selfridges in 1930, the Queen of Time, dressed in glorious Art Deco lapis blue-and-bronze robes, looks proudly down on shoppers below. More than three metres tall, she stands at the prow of the (stone) ship of commerce, topped by a double-faced clock, flanked by bronze-and-mosaic (rather masculine) mermaids and backed by a couple of angels. Above and below are more conventional symbolic female figures, but the *Queen of Time* undoubtedly commands.

Despite her allegorical idealisation, the Queen's face is not that of a lifeless figurehead – which is perhaps what prompted Lucy Merello Peterson's quest (described in her book *The Women Who Inspired London Art*) to uncover her identity. More than 90 years after the Queen's creation, Peterson discovered that the model was Leopoldine Avico (1907–79) – and this wasn't her only statue.

Brought up near Oxford Street, 'Leo' was the middle of three sisters, with an adored baby brother.

Their Italian father died in an asylum in 1914, and their second 'Daddy' succumbed to TB three years later. Their French mother tried to support them, but sometimes had to sign her children temporarily into the local workhouse. They always came back together, however, and on a cold afternoon in 1918 an artist (identity unknown) spotted the four siblings on Tottenham Court Road and asked their mother if he could draw them.

The children were strikingly attractive in

a way that suited contemporary
taste, and in 1923 the London
Daily News described them as
'living perfections'. Leo grew
into a professional artists' model
and, following a failed marriage,
brought up her own son alone on
her earnings.

She modelled for life classes
at the Slade art school until
at least the late 1950s, and Art
Deco sculptors immortalised
her not only at Selfridges but as
the spirit of wine on Vintner's
Place (in the quarter of the City
associated for centuries with the
wine trade). In contrast to the
traditional allegorical females
adorning Vintner's Hall next door
(made only 15 years earlier), Leo's
Bacchante stands in full-frontal
nakedness (though without
pubic hair), grinning down at
us, innocently or suggestively
depending on your view. I'm
going for innocent; her grin here
is almost identical to that in her
childhood photos, presumably
the look that attracted artists to
her in the first place.

Laid bare (or, what's with all the naked women?)

When Maggi Hambling's monument to Mary Wollstonecraft (p. 128) was unveiled in 2020, the writer Tracy King (who had been part of the campaign for Millicent Fawcett's statue in Parliament Square, p. 134) told the *Guardian*, 'Any passing teenage boy is not going to think, "Oh, that's an icon of feminist education." They are going to think, "Tits!"'

This is nothing new. Hambling's figure stands in a long and venerable line of 'tits!' statues ranged across London. Indeed, they appear on some of our most serious buildings, including the Supreme Court (p. 178), the Old Bailey (p. 90) and the Foreign Office (where the personifications of America and Africa are uncomfortably more naked than Europe). Many are Victorian or Edwardian – periods known for public prudery – and 'justify' their nudity or semi-nudity through stylistic and titular (sorry) classical allusion.

Take *Charity* (1910) on Bethnal Green Town Hall, with the face of an Edwardian lady but pert bare breasts, and her legs wide apart (albeit draped), in

Africa, Foreign & Commonwealth Office, Whitehall facade statues, Portland stone. Archtect: George Gilbert Scott. Sculptor: John Birnie Phiip (1824–75).

Charity, Bethnal Green Town Hall (now Town Hall Hotel), Cambridge Heath Rd (corner of Patriot Square), E2 9NF. Portland stone, 1910. By Henry Poole (1873–1928).

a pose for which any girl of the time would have been roundly ticked off. Or Chelsea Embankment's *Atalanta* (1907, placed here 1929), a Greek mythological virgin huntress who rejected the attention of men (what could be more alluring?). This silky, hairless beauty, arms raised to perfectly display her naked body, even has nipples erect. She is clearly intended to arouse.

More naturalistic but still posed erotically is nearby *Awakening* (1915, now in Roper's Garden). This nude

is shown 'stretching from sleep', a theme also deployed on the Strand's Australia House (1915–18) with similarly erotic results. This raised no objections, but just a few years earlier Jacob Epstein's nudes for the British Medical Association building (now Zimbabwe House) also on the Strand, caused uproar.

The *Evening Standard* opined that naked figures in an art gallery were OK because they were seen only by the educated, but to have art of this kind 'laid bare to the gaze of all classes, young and old, in perhaps the busiest thoroughfare of the Metropolis of the world, is a different matter'. Naturally, this drew crowds to see what all the fuss was about.

Most of the art world jumped to Epstein's defence, but the naysayers got their way in the end. In 1937 the head fell off one of the figures, providing a 'safety first' excuse to mutilate the rest. The Royal Academy failed to protest, and Henry Moore (p. 114) consequently refused ever to exhibit there again.

Epstein's 'crime' was to put realism before beauty (male and female). Classical and Renaissance sculptors depicted both sexes in idealised nakedness, but nineteenth- to twenty-first-century statuary has been less egalitarian. Naked sexy men are unusual in London's public sculpture, and it is hard to imagine a male equivalent of Mary Wollstonecraft (Rousseau, perhaps, or Hobbes?) memorialised with a fit nude.

Unless of course it was a female nude representing the male master's muse, skill or virtue. Arthur

top: One of Jacob Epstein's mutilated nudes, Zimbabwe House (British Medical Association HQ at time of commission), 429 Strand, WC2R 0JR. Stone, 1908.

above: *The Awakening of Australia*, Australia House, Strand. By Harold Parker, stone, 1915–18.

Sullivan (of Gilbert and . . .), commemorated in Victoria Embankment Gardens (c. 1903), stares resolutely ahead, while a 'mourning' near-naked nymph clings to his plinth apparently helpless with ecstasy. Close by, Samuel Plimsoll (of the Plimsoll ship-loading line, 1928–9) is flanked by a topless female Justice (see also p. 90), while military and municipal memorials regularly feature 'tits!' women personifying Victory or Peace (see also p. 194).

There is sometimes iconographical logic to nudity. Breastfeeding has long been a symbol of caring and charity,

top: Arthur Sullivan memorial, Victoria Embankment Gardens, WC2N 6PB. Bronze, 1903. By William Goscombe John.

above: *La Délivrance*, Regents Park Road (just north of the North Circular), N3 3JH. Bronze, 1914; in this location from 1927. By Émile Guillaume.

right: The Sunbathers. On a vertical wall, upper level, Waterloo Station. Terracotta, 1952, restored and reinstalled here 2020. By Peter Laszlo Peri.

far right: Broadgate Venus, Exchange Square, EC2A 2BQ. Bronze, 1989. By Fernando Botero (b. 1932).

and Truth is symbolically naked or laid bare. The latter, though, does not necessitate a female body, and neither requires a come-hither pose.

Not all unclothed female statues pander so transparently to the 'male gaze'. *La Délivrance* (next to a main road in Finchley) is fully naked but has a naturalness, sense of motion and agency that make her attractive without being pornographic. Created in 1914 to celebrate victory in that year's battle to keep the Germans out of Paris, the figure is more 1920s swimmer than erotic model, more *Girl with a Dolphin* (1973, p. 68) than *Atalanta*, and imparts an appropriate sense of freedom.

The Wollstonecraft controversy notwithstanding, times have changed. The mere fact that there was

controversy is indicative, and it is difficult to imagine how the Edwardians might have reacted, for instance, to the five tons of confident bronze voluptuousness that is the *Broadgate Venus* (Fernando Bolero, 1989) or the matter-of-factness of the South Bank's *London Pride* (p. 73). Naked or semi-naked couples have colonised the city too. All different but mostly sympathetic, and presenting a welcome egalitarianism between the sexes. They range from Waterloo Station's terracotta *Sunbathers* and Hyde Park's uplifting *Joy of Life* fountain to the City's *Beyond Tomorrow* and *Young Lovers*.

There's nothing wrong with nudity in statues, as in life. But as in life, so in statues, it depends on the context and intent.

Louisa Brandreth Aldrich-Blake Stone and bronze, 1926

Louisa Brandreth Aldrich-Blake (1865–1925) commands the south-east corner of Tavistock Square, her monument's double-sided bust on her monument looking both ways. As the first fully qualified female surgeon, she may have needed eyes in the back of her head.

She presents a confident figure, arms folded, book in hand, staring on one side over a high hedge to the pavement and traffic beyond, on the other across the square's peaceful gardens towards the headquarters of the British Medical Association, of which she was an influential member.

It is easier to see her from the garden side, and this is the only place from which to read the otherwise twig-tangled plinth detailing her pioneering senior surgical and teaching positions at the Royal Free and Elizabeth Garrett Anderson hospitals (both then nearby).

The second of six children of a comfortably off Essex clergyman, Aldrich-Blake graduated from medical school in 1894. Just a year later she became the first woman to gain a Master of Surgery degree, and by 1910 she was a lead surgeon and anaesthetist.

The first person in Britain to carry out operations for cervical and rectal cancers, the paper detailing her new surgical technique was published by the *British Medical Journal* in 1903.

During World War I Aldrich-Blake was personally responsible for doubling the number of female

students at the Royal Free Medical School for Women, of which she was Dean, and she wrote to every woman on the medical register, recruiting many to serve in the Royal Army Medical Corps in Egypt, Malta and Greece. She spent her own holidays treating the wounded, particularly in France, where patients called her 'Madame la Générale'.

In 1925 she was made a Dame of the British Empire shortly before she died of cancer. It is a measure of the esteem in which she was held that this memorial was erected the following year, with a curved stone seat designed by the leading architect of the day, Sir Edwin Lutyens.

Margaret MacDonald Bronze, 1914

By Richard Reginald Goulden
Lincoln's Inn Fields, WC2A 3BP

This charming bronze of Margaret MacDonald (1870–1911), arms stretched protectively around nine lively cherubs, commemorates a social reformer, Suffragist and mother of six. The statue's bronze infants arrive at her (left) side seeking comfort before dancing happily off into their future.

It is hard to avoid the ungenerous thought that this monument might not exist had Margaret not been the wife of three-times prime minister Ramsay MacDonald, but she died ten years before he became PM and it was her friends who raised the funds for this statue. Ramsay certainly approved, and the monument stands close to their marital home at 3 Lincoln's Inn Fields, but this tribute is on her own merit.

Born in London to a comfortably off family of scientists, Margaret Gladstone (no relation to the earlier PM) quickly became involved in social work with deprived families. In 1894 she joined the Women's Industrial Council and, also a member of the Royal Statistical Society, led research into conditions for female 'home workers' and London barmaids. She was central to the founding of the first trade schools for girls.

Margaret held leadership positions in several reformist organisations including the Women's Labour League and Millicent Fawcett's (p. 134) Suffragist organisation (she did not approve of the Pankhursts' methods, p. 64).

Through her work Margaret met the Labour politician Ramsay MacDonald, the illegitimate son of a Scottish farm labourer and a housemaid.

They married in 1896 and had six children.

Evidently it was a very happy family until the death of one of their sons, followed by Margaret's own demise from sepsis at just 41. She left five children, from newborn to age 13, and a grieving husband.

A year after her death, Ramsay published a loving, admiring biography of his wife, celebrating her joie de vivre and unforced empathy and 'an attractively strange mixture of childlike innocence and mature

commonsense'.

Their oldest daughter, Ishbel, who had attended her first suffrage march with her mother aged four, became her father's political hostess while he was PM from 1924, despite not being entitled to vote until 1928.

This statue might seem a rather sentimental rendition of this remarkable woman, her attire a little too 'allegorical', but her face is individual and sympathetic and, compared with the formality of the very few contemporary public statues of women – Florence Nightingale (p. 66), Edith Cavell (p. 58) – the monument has a welcome, and by all accounts appropriate, vitality and warmth.

St Mary, the Madonna

The Virgin Mary is the most ubiquitous female saint, and a powerful – and equivocal – contributor to ideas of femininity. Though she was a real person (if Jesus was, so was his mother), that is not where her importance lies. A perplexing combination of virgin and mother, she has often been enlisted to sideline and even demonise independent womanhood and female sexuality. Few women would want her life (loss of agency, only son crucified), but she is Christianity's ultimate female role model.

More Church of England churches are dedicated to the Virgin Mary than to any other saint, man or woman, and among female saints only she and St Mary Magdalene (p. 112) have a significant presence among London's public statues.

The Virgin Mary frequently appears on churches with baby Jesus, mostly in conventional Victorian images of the pacific mother and upright Christ child, perhaps with his hand raised in blessing. The Madonna also appears alone, and sometimes in unexpected locations – over the door of student accommodation (Lillian Knowles House, E1 6HQ), or above an alley near Oxford Street (see below) – though these are usually because the buildings were once convents. In the twentieth century Mary has also been sculpted in more varied ways.

A sweet-faced, almost childlike Madonna holds baby Jesus above the door of this pretty little 1816 church, founded by a refugee priest from revolutionary

France. It was the first post-Reformation Catholic church in Hampstead village (then actually a village), and was probably named after the first known chapel in Hampstead, a tenth-century St Mary's built by monks of Westminster Abbey (p. 26 and p. 132). The Virgin and Child was added along with the bell tower in 1850 in celebration of a change in the law that allowed Catholic churches to ring bells for the first time since the Reformation.

Madonna and Child

Designed by George Gilbert Scott (then the abbey surveyor); carved by Messrs Farmer & Brindley, 1885

Westminster Abbey

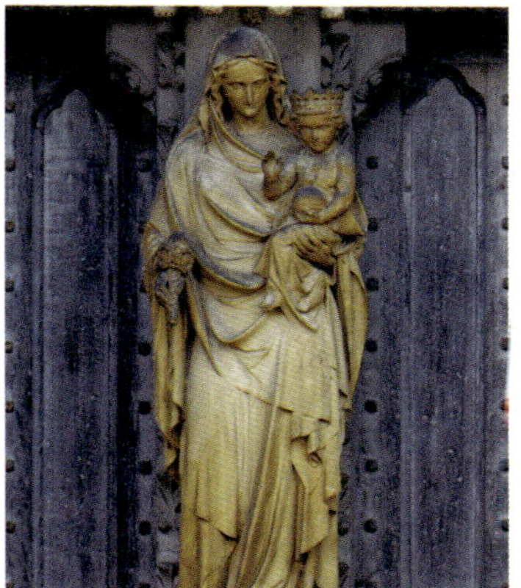

A conventional, well-made Victorian Virgin and Child blessing the comings and goings through the abbey's North door.

Virgin Mary

Unknown artist, 1868

Lilian Knowles House, 50 Crispin St, E1 6HQ

A lone, rather melancholy young Madonna stands above the door of student accommodation named after a female economist. The building was the Convent of Mercy.

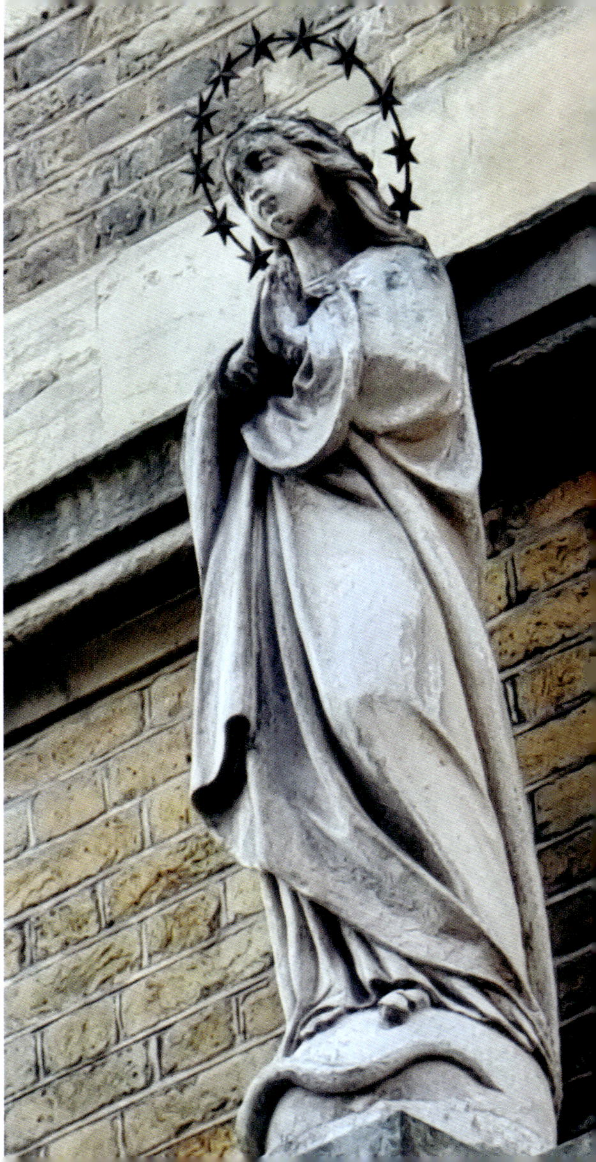

Mary of Nazareth Stone, 1925

By Charles Wheeler (see also p. 80-2); placed here in the sculptor's memory, 1975

Grounds of St James's Piccadilly, W1J 9LL

This flowing figure, often thought to be a young Mary pre-Jesus, stands alone, attentive, hands raised as if listening or surprised, her toe tucked over the edge of the pedestal. Her forward-curving body, raised hands and uncertain expression have been interpreted as a response to the annunciation.

Madonna and Child Lead, 1953

By Jacob Epstein

On bridge over Dean's Mews, north side of Cavendish Square, W1G 0AN

A stone's throw from Oxford Street, this unusual Madonna and Child now seems rather out of place, but it was commissioned during the post-war reconstruction of the Convent of the Holy Child Jesus which occupied the buildings either side. A controversial Jewish artist (see p. 101-2), Epstein was a difficult sell to the nuns, and the architect Louis Osman had to employ a little subterfuge and a lot of persuasion. At the sculpture's unveiling, however, the response was overwhelmingly positive, and this remains a striking, evocative and unsentimental image. The mother's hands do not touch the child she cannot protect, while the Christ child's pose throws us forward to the crucifixion.

St Mary Magdalene St Lawrence & St Mary Magdelene drinking fountain

Mary Magdalene is the most mentioned female name in the gospels outside Jesus's family, and is believed to have been a real person. She may have hailed from Magdala Nunaya, a fishing town on the Sea of Galilee, but little is known of her life. In the Bible she is present at the crucifixion and resurrection, travels with the disciples as a follower of Jesus and is the closest woman to him besides his mother (Mary, the Madonna, p. 108).

The two Marys are an interesting pair: the virgin and the prostitute, the virtuous and the (albeit penitent) sinner. Poor Mary M. There is actually no biblical reference to her as sinful (let alone a sex worker), unless by inference from Jesus ridding her of 'seven demons'. Her characterisation as a 'fallen woman' dates to the sixth century and Pope Gregory I ('the Great').

Gregory and the Catholic Church conflated Mary Magdalene with other biblical women, particularly the unnamed 'sinful woman' who wept over Jesus's feet and then wiped them with her hair – which explains the long flowing locks on her statues. The same woman then anointed Jesus with perfumes – hence the ointment jar that often accompanies Mary (including at Munster Square and Brockley).

In 1969 the Vatican quietly set aside Gregory's

Munster Square

Mortlake

Brockley

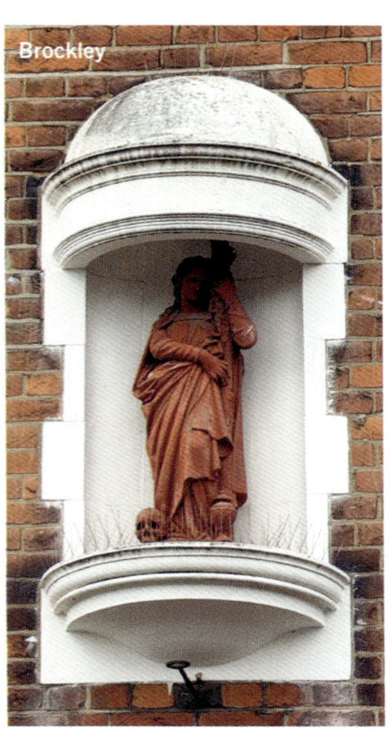

characterisation. Too quietly – 1,400 years confers a lot of consolidation on an image propagated through art, literature and the pulpit. In the public mind Mary Magdalene remains the patron saint of sex workers and penitent sinners.

'That may be inaccurate and unfair', says Fr Adrian McKenna of St Mary Magdalen, Mortlake, 'but it has been useful'. A redeemed sinner sends a powerful message, and St Mary M. has encouraged the Church to reach out to the abused and socially outcast, he says, especially women.

Modern ministry, however, concentrates on her biblically clear closeness to Christ, and status as the first to whom he spoke after the resurrection (John 20:11–18), which makes her, Fr McKenna adds, a very important saint – again, especially for women.

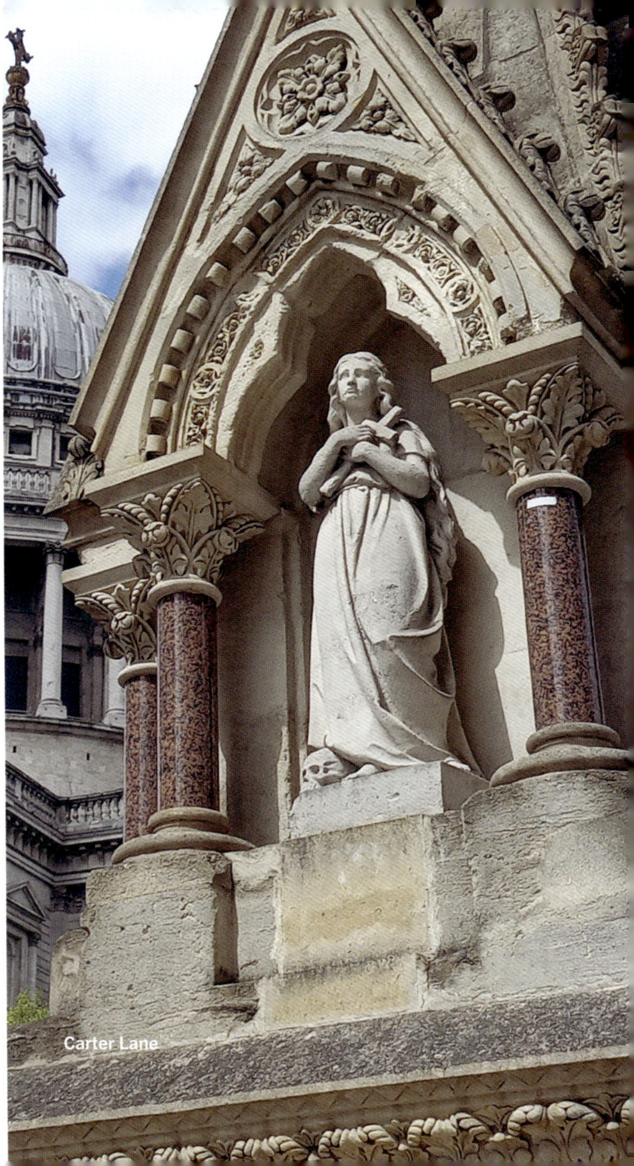
Carter Lane

Henry Moore's London Women

Three Standing Figures

Though only one of Henry Moore's London women is titled as such, all these works are near-universally accepted as female. 'Right from the beginning', said Moore, the most famous British sculptor of the twentieth century and a prolific maker of public art,

'I have been more interested in the female form than in the male. Nearly all my drawings and virtually all my sculptures are based on the female form.'

Three, arguably four, of Moore's London women belong to the same series, and I used to find these divided, distorted, abstracted *Two Piece Reclining Figures* a bit cold and impenetrable. That was until I understood Moore's interest in geology, and especially his intense wartime experiences as a soldier during the First World War and an official artist in the Second.

Moore himself said that these works – which vary enormously according to your viewing angle – allowed him to combine the body and landscape, or as some commentators have put it, the mother and Mother Earth.

Two Piece No. 5 (Kenwood) – one of the easier pieces to interpret as an abstracted, fragmented woman – was originally an alternative model for his 1961 commission for New York's Lincoln Center. The finished work was rather different and designed to sit surrounded by water, as it now does in NYC and (half-size) outside London's Charing Cross Hospital. Moore said his one represents a woman and a rock.

Moore's lifelong interest in reclining female figures arose, he explained, from 1,000-year-old Mexican art in the British Museum, specifically Chacmool sculptures – sacred (male) figures with bulky bodies and upright heads turned 90°. Moore liked their mass and solidity, though this characteristic of his women

Two Piece Reclining Figure No. 1

Two Piece Reclining Figure No. 5

Two Piece Reclining Figure No. 3

their day-to-day lives. *Two Piece Reclining Figure No.3* sits surrounded by tower blocks on a South London council estate, while *Draped Seated Woman* was installed on an East End estate in 1958, where she became affectionately known as Old Flo.

Exiled to Yorkshire following the estate's demolition in 1997, she survived a controversial attempt to sell her to plug a Tower Hamlets budget shortfall, before returning to the borough in 2017. Now on corporate land, she is nonetheless visible to all, semi-recumbent on her bronze bench, solid but not settled, a precursor to Moore's more abstract reclining figures to come.

(as well as their 3D poetic licence) he also credited to the sculptural 'monumentality' and 'strength' he saw in Cezanne's *The Bathers* and works by Picasso.

Three Standing Figures, the earliest of Moore's London women, has a certain peace and timeless classicism (the art historian Will Grohmann wrote in 1960 that the trio had 'something of the prophetess about them'). The figures derive from Moore's evocative wartime drawings of people swathed in blankets, sheltering from air raids in the London Underground, but the artist said that while the shelter drawings sought to convey 'communion in apprehension', he wanted only 'a hint of that mood' here, overlayed with 'a sense of release . . . [the] figures conscious of being in the open air'.

Moore believed sculpture to be an 'open-air art', and nature its best setting. Much of his work, though, is in urban spaces, partly because he also believed in placing art where 'ordinary' people would see in

Draped Seated Woman

La Parra Tapas
Bury
FOOD & WINE
LITTER
Reclining Figure

Mary Poppins and Wonder Woman Bronze, 2020

By Samantha Wild

Scenes on the Square, Leicester Square, WC2H 7DE (Mary Poppins west side, Wonder Woman on the side of the Vue West End cinema just off the square in Leicester Court).

Mary Poppins lands neatly on a flower bed in Leicester Square, the umbrella that is her aerial propulsion poised above her head. A rare monument to a fictional female, she nonetheless slots into the inventory of women memorialised in London. So too, in a different way, does her companion piece, Wonder Woman, who bursts, minimally dressed, from the side of a cinema building just off the square.

Both are powerful female 'ideals'. Mary Poppins, in Disney's magical 1964 film (from P. L. Travers' classic novel), is the super-nanny who gently manipulates the Banks family into harmony, before she selflessly flies away to do the same elsewhere.

Wonder Woman, on the other hand, is a modern take on that age-old male fantasy, the sexy female warrior. Her 1941 creator, the American psychologist William Moulton Marston (encouraged by his bisexual psychologist wife), intended her as a liberated woman. 'Frankly, Wonder Woman is psychological propaganda for the new type of woman who, I believe, should rule the world,' he said, 'Not even girls want to be girls so long as our feminine archetype lacks force, strength and power . . . The obvious remedy is to create a feminine character with all the strength of Superman plus all the allure of a good and beautiful woman.'

Linked to mythology from her inception, Wonder Woman in this bronze looks like a twenty-first-century iteration of the similarly pert-breasted allegorical statues of Victory, Honour, Justice et al. that dot war memorials, public buildings and

monuments to military men across London (p. 102, 122).

Poppins and Wonder Woman are the only females among the 12 *Scenes on the Square* statues of film characters erected in 2020–4 to celebrate Leicester Square's long association with the silver screen. The first cinema here opened in 1930, and the first 'red carpet' premier soon followed.

Though supposed to be a tribute to the five-Oscar-winning, box-office-record-breaking Disney film, this Mary Poppins looks nothing like Julie Andrews in her first feature film role, and much more like Zizi Stallen, who was playing Poppins in the West End when the statue was created.

Wonder Woman, another flyer, is encircled by her 'lasso of truth', here a curling neon tube (best seen at night) winding about her like a combination of halo and weapon – naturally used only for virtuous purposes.

Mary Queen of Scots Stone, 1905

Architect Richard Mauleverer Roe,
sculptor unknown

Mary Queen of Scots House (above
Prêt à Manger), 143–4 Fleet St, EC4A 2BP

Looking down on us from above a branch of Prêt à Manger, this rather romanticised Mary, Queen of Scots (1542–87) adorns a Neo-Gothic filigree façade designed by a Scottish architect for a Scottish insurance company in 1905. The statue was commissioned by the developer, Sir John Tollemache Sinclair MP, another Scot, with a passion for the queen. An early proponent of disc recordings, in 1906 he even recorded a poem about her.

Mary became queen of Scotland at six days old when her father, James V, died. Throughout babyhood she was moved pillar-to-post evading the English. Henry VIII wanted her married to his son Edward (VI-to-be), by force if necessary. Instead, aged five, Mary was betrothed to the sickly toddler dauphin Francis and moved to France. Her French mother stayed behind to mind the Scottish crown, but Mary took along four little friends – all called Mary.

In 1559, the 15-year-old Francis became King of France, making Mary a double queen. But he soon died, and the tall, attractive, Catholic, 18-year-old widow queen – or 'silly, idle, coquettish French girl', as some Scots saw her – was packed off back to Scotland.

Mary's Protestant cousin Elizabeth I now sat on the English throne and tension between Protestants and Catholics was not helped by Mary marrying

another cousin, handsome, arrogant, Catholic Lord Darnley. He was soon involved in killing Mary's private secretary – in front of the pregnant queen – and, shortly after the birth of their son James, Darnley was himself murdered. Suspicion fell on Mary, and on her

(Protestant and unpopular) friend Lord Bothwell – soon to be Mary's third husband.

Imprisoned and forced to abdicate, Mary escaped to England (maybe not a good choice). Cousin Elizabeth had made friendly noises, but was afraid of Mary's Catholicism and claim to the English throne. Mary lived under house arrest for eighteen and a half years before Elizabeth reluctantly (regicide not setting a good example) had her beheaded for treason. But there's a coda: when Elizabeth died childless, Mary's son, James VI of Scotland, became James I of England.

Violent whore or pious martyr, traitor or victim, Mary has always captured the public imagination. Called 'poor Mary' by Queen Victoria (p. 164), she fascinated more than just Tollemache. Nonetheless, at its installation this improbably serene effigy of a woman who lived such a tumultuous life was the UK's only outdoor statue of the queen. Scotland finally gained one in 2015.

Musing on Muses

Tucked between ill-lit concrete walkways in a corner of the labyrinthine Barbican Centre dangles an almost Buddha-like golden female. Commissioned for the 1993–4 refurbishment of the centre, Zoe the Barbican Muse – holding the masks of theatre – was intended to 'float, glow and point the way' to the arts from Moorgate Station.

Named after the Cambridge University student who posed for the figure, Zoe was originally the tenth muse to a group of nine gilded fibreglass figures above the Silk Street entrance. These, however, were deemed too kitsch – a previous artistic director described them as 'tatty, gold-plated, big-breasted statues', good for nothing but target practice – and they were removed after just three years. Zoe alone survived. Tenth was always a strange status: in classical mythology there were no more than nine muses. Daughters of Zeus and Mnemosyne (Memory), they were the goddesses of inspiration.

Classical writers gave them various names and roles, but from the Renaissance onwards they acquired more consistent identities and attributes. Euterpe, goddess of instrumental music, for instance, often holds a double pipe, as she does atop the doorway of Frank Matcham's Richmond Theatre (TW9 1QJ, by John Broad, 1899). She also stands more or less life size in warm terracotta in St George's Gardens, Bloomsbury (WC1N 1PG, 1898), sole public survivor of the nine sisters that once adorned the Apollo Inn on Tottenham Court Road (demolished).

Muses – usually semi-naked – are found adorning memorials to their artistic masters, including Arthur Sullivan

Zoe, Barbican Muse, by Matthew Spender (b. 1945). Polyurethane, glass fibre and gold leaf, 1994.

(p. 102) and sculptor Edward Onslow Ford (NW8 9DE, 1903). Ford's muse, though, is not related to the visual arts, but a copy of the muse of lyric poetry (holding a lyre) that he made for the Oxford memorial to the poet Percy Bysshe Shelley.

The Muses' greatest impact on London's streets, however, is not as themselves, but as

above: Muse on Memorial to Edward Onslow Ford RA. Junction of Abbey Rd/Grove End Rd, NW8 9DE (near his home at 62 Acacia Rd), 1903 copy of Onslow Ford's 1893 Shelley Muse of Poetry.

right: Euterpe, Richmond Theatre

inspiration for the innumerable female personifications of a vast range of – almost always masculine – achievements and skills.

Take the pediment on the archetypal Neoclassical façade of the British Museum ('museum' meaning place of muse-worship). Filled with Greek-style statues, it narrates the civilisation of man (last work of the accomplished Richard Westmacott, 1848-52), From the left corner, an early human (male) emerges to discover

hunting and farming before reaching the first of seven muse-like personifications of creative/knowledge-based pursuits – six of them female. Architecture, Sculpture and Painting lead to the upright central figure of Astronomy/Science who, like her origin muse Urania, clutches a globe. Next to her is Mathematics – the only male – then drama and music. In the right-hand corner reclines a 'civilised' modern man. Of course: man. All these

above: British Museum Pediment, by Richard Westmacott, Portland stone, 1848–52

left: Euterpe, St George's Gardens

women help him to get there, but it is he that arrives.

Such personifications pepper the façades of public buildings (see Supreme Court, p. 178) and statues of 'Great Men' across the capital. William Gladstone, for instance, towers in bronze above the Strand surrounded by women representing Education, Aspiration, Courage and Brotherhood (yes, Brotherhood). On such memorials, Muses often merge with Virtues – also classical females, but with a different provenance. The Greek philosophers Plato and Aristotle named the Cardinal Virtues: Prudence, Fortitude, Temperance (see also p. 32) and Justice (p. 90). The Christian Church later added Faith, Hope and Charity/Love. Victorian and Edwardian artists happily mashed them all up and adapted them to their own purposes.

Nearly a century younger, Zoe is classically draped and semi-naked, but otherwise quite different. This glittering six-metre muse hangs from cables like a displaced pantomime flyer or mega-premium party balloon, pointing a little desperately along the Brutalist walkway to the door of the Barbican's 'temple of the arts'.

William Gladstone with Education (NB educating a male child), in front of St Clement Danes Church, Strand, WC2R 1DH by William Hamo Thornycroft, 1904. The memorial also includes female personifications of Courage, Aspiration and Brotherhood (and children — all male).

Mary Seacole Bronze, 2016

By Martin Jennings

The Queen's Walk, SE1 7GA. Outside St Thomas' Hospital, east end of Westminster Bridge

As the twenty-first century took off, the UK seemed to go mad for Mary Seacole (1805–81). She ticked all the boxes for righting historic wrongs of under-representation: a woman of colour and healthcare heroine fallen into obscurity. In 2004 Seacole topped the first poll for Greatest Black Briton, in 2007 she was added to the National Curriculum, in 2013 a 2D portrait sculpture was erected at St Mary's Paddington Green (p. 184), and in 2016 this striking 4.9-metre monument was unveiled outside St Thomas' Hospital.

The location was perhaps an odd choice; Seacole had no connection with 'Tommy's', whereas her Crimean War nursing contemporary Florence Nightingale (p. 66) founded the world's first modern nursing school here. Nightingale now stands on the Crimean War Memorial on Waterloo Place. They should really swap places. But let's not quibble. This is a dramatic modern monument to a remarkable woman. Set at ground level, the larger-than-life figure strides confidently, determinedly forward in solid boots, bag slung over her shoulder, the world her oyster.

Seacole was certainly confident and determined – and adventurous. 'No sooner had I heard of war somewhere', she said, 'than I longed to witness it.' Born in Jamaica in 1905 to a white Scottish army officer and a Creole Jamaican traditional 'doctress', by the age of 12 Mary was helping her mother run a boarding house and care for sick soldiers. She travelled from an early age, to England, Cuba,

Haiti and the Bahamas. The 1840s saw her lose her husband, mother and home (to fire) before nursing victims of cholera epidemics in Kingston and Panama.

Refusing to remarry, she devoted herself to travel, business and nursing. It was speculation on the Californian Gold Rush that brought her to London in

1854, but she soon became
obsessed with getting to
Crimea to help save soldiers
dying in their droves from
disease. Having failed to find
an official position, despite
petitioning the War Office
and Nightingale herself,
Seacole went it alone.
Travelling to Crimea (where
she had military and medical
contacts from Kingston
days), she set up a store and
restaurant to make money,
and nursed wherever she
saw the need – and there was
enormous need.

In his introduction to
Seacole's 1857 autobiography,
the *Times* Crimean War
correspondent, William
Howard Russell, wrote,
'I trust that England will not
forget one who nursed her
sick, who sought out her
wounded to aid and succour
them, and who performed
the last offices for some of
her illustrious dead.' It did –
but it doesn't any more.

Mary Wollstonecraft Bronze (coloured silver), 2020

By Maggi Hambling

Newington Green, N16 9PR

See also: Maggi Hambling interview (p.130), Laid Bare (p. 100)

There were high hopes for this monument, commissioned from a leading female artist by a female-led committee that had raised £143,300 for the purpose. Unveiled, however, it met with some consternation, especially among women. The plinth

carries Mary Wollstonecraft's (1759–97) most famous line – 'I do not wish women to have power over men but over themselves' – but many felt the sculpture had little connection with one of our first feminist

writers – indeed, one of the first British women to make her name as a writer at all.

Its creator, Maggi Hambling, says the statue is 'of an idea . . . an everywoman' rising from a mass of 'mingling female forms', representing the struggle from which Wollstonecraft and feminism emerged. Today's women, first beholding this small, gym-muscled silver nude, weren't all convinced. 'Imagine', tweeted the feminist writer Caitlin Moran, 'if there was a statue of a hot young naked guy "in tribute" to e.g. Churchill . . .'

The sculpture stands opposite London's oldest surviving non-conformist place of worship, Newington Green Unitarian Church, which Wollstonecraft attended with the 'rationalist dissenters'. She briefly ran a girls' boarding school nearby, seeing education as central to women's rights.

Best known for her *A Vindication of the Rights of Woman* (1792), she made her name with *A Vindication of the Rights of Men* (1790), a passionate defence of the previous year's French Revolution. Wollstonecraft moved to Paris in late 1792 and lived through the Terror, losing friends to the guillotine. She declared it nightmarish but intellectually challenging.

Wollstonecraft knew both wealth and poverty, abuse and liberation. She attempted suicide twice, and had three long-term relationships with interesting (but not necessarily reliable) men. She had a child with two, but married only one, the radical political philosopher William Godwin. This was a marriage of minds and mutual respect, but after just six months Wollstonecraft died of postpartum sepsis after giving birth to their daughter, who grew up to be Mary Shelley, author of *Frankenstein* (1818).

The heartbroken Godwin wrote a tell-all memoir intended as a tribute to his extraordinary wife, and it caused a scandal from which Wollstonecraft's reputation only recovered with the advent of modern feminism. In the meantime, she influenced radical women like the Suffragist Millicent Fawcett (p. 134), and female writers from Jane Austen to Virginia Woolf (p. 202).

Controversy, then, is part of Mary Wollstonecraft's story, and the debate around this statue has certainly raised awareness of the remarkable woman it commemorates.

An Interview with Maggi Hambling

Are there any statues of women in London you particularly admire?

Nothing comes to mind . . . I think Nelson's column is wonderful – our hero Nelson towering even over the National Gallery.

What about the Millicent Fawcett statue in Parliament Square?

No comment . . . You see, the moment the person is clothed in the dress of their period, it defines them, limits them, sticks them into history. They're just another old statue people walk past. It was very important to me with Mary Wollstonecraft that it was about now. So there is a tower of the trials and tribulations of history and this woman at the top, defiant. The scale is important. The figure is only about a foot high – a small part of the sculpture.

Do you think that because the statue commemorates an individual, people tend to focus on the figure and miss the broader sculpture?

Yes. Annoyingly, the photographs in the media mostly only showed the nude, as if it was the whole statue.

Even so, there has been naked statuary forever. I really don't know what all the fuss was about or why the feminists took against it in such a big way. Do they not have bodies?

Maybe not that kind of body? You've called this an everywoman, but she's very fit, in both senses of the word – and Wollstonecraft complained about women being judged on their appearance.

It's important she is up there confidently challenging, finally there after all the trials and tribulations. It's a statue *for* Mary Wollstonecraft, not of her. For her spirit. And she was actually quite a goer herself!

During the fuss following the unveiling, my friend, the writer Paul Bailey, rang me (before I took the phone off the hook) and said, 'You've really put the pussy among the pigeons this time!' – my favourite comment on it all.

You certainly got people talking.

Not deliberately. I don't set out to be controversial, but there seems to be a fuss whenever I do public sculpture. It was the same with *Oscar Wilde* [1998, WC2N 4HZ] and *Scallop* on Aldeburgh beach [2003,

commemorating Benjamin Britten]. I was a bit upset about that; I thought it was one of the more beautiful things I'd made. Now it seems to be popular. People get married there, and I've even had letters from people asking permission to fire their ashes from it – I said fine!

It must be quite different making a public statue from painting freely in your studio?

Not really. I've never felt restricted. I've always done

what I want. Then committees choose – except the *Scallop*; we raised the money for that. Some people like my work, some hate it. I can't help that. I make it, it goes out into the world.

The difference is in how people see them. Paintings are safely on a wall in a gallery. You can choose to look at them or not, whereas public sculpture confronts you – it inhabits your space.

Modern Martyrs French Richemont limestone, 1998

On the Gothic façade of London's greatest historic church you might expect to find female saints or personifications of virtue, but above the Great West Door of Westminster Abbey there's something less expected: ten statues of twentieth-century Christian martyrs, three of them women, two women of colour.

The niches are fifteenth century, but only in the 1990s were they finally filled. The unveiling was attended by Queen Elizabeth II (p. 160) and Prince Philip, respectively a cousin and grand-nephew of 'modern martyr' Grand Duchess Elizabeth of Russia (1864–1918).

A grand-daughter of Queen Victoria, and a renowned beauty, Elizabeth of Hesse married Grand-Duke Sergei Alexandrovich, fifth son of Tsar Alexander II. After her husband's 1905 assassination by a socialist revolutionary, Elizabeth sold all her jewellery (even her wedding ring) and founded the St Martha and Mary Convent in Moscow, dedicating her life to the sick and poor.

In 1918 she was arrested by the Bolsheviks, and the day after the execution of the Tsar and Tsarina (Elizabeth's sister), Elizabeth too was murdered. 'Virtue with the crown on it is a greater enemy to world revolution than a hundred tyrant tsars,' said Lenin. In 1981 she became a saint of the Russian Orthodox Church.

Manche Masemola (1913–28) never had expensive jewellery. A poor Pedi girl from what is now north-

eastern Johannesburg, she became involved with the local Christian mission. Having failed to detach their child from this alien religion, her parents took her to a remote spot and killed her. Her rocky grave became a pilgrimage site, and in 1969 her mother was baptised. 1975 saw Masemola's name added to the liturgical calendar of the Southern African Anglican Church.

Born a Muslim in India, Qamar Zia (1929–60) was introduced to the Bible at school and developed a devotion to Christianity. Leaving home to avoid an arranged Muslim marriage, she worked in a missionary orphanage in Karachi, where she was given the name Esther John. Her family never accepted her Christianity, but she settled in the Punjab, cycling around the villages teaching women to read and evangelising – until she was found murdered in her bed.

To those outside the Christian Church (and perhaps some within) the idolisation of these 'martyrs' might feel less than 'modern'. Grand Duchess Elizabeth and Qamar/Esther can at least be seen to have helped others – especially women. Masemola's story, however, seems more sorrowful than inspiring. These women's effigies nonetheless add to the complex, millennium-spanning web of stories held within the fabric of this extraordinary church.

Millicent Fawcett Bronze, 2018

By Gillian Wearing RA

Parliament Square, SW1P 3BD

Nearby: Emmeline Pankhurst, Suffragette (p. 64)
See also Interview with Gillian Wearing about making this statue – p. 136

Flanked by the Houses of Parliament, the Treasury, Westminster Abbey (p. 36, p. 132) and the Supreme Court (p. 178), and at the heart of 'the Establishment', Parliament Square is the most politically important location in London. Its statuary has long been dominated by British elder statesmen, though in the twentieth century it gained Nelson Mandela and Mahatma Gandhi. Until 2018, however, women were conspicuous by their absence.

Or perhaps not conspicuous enough. So accustomed were we to the masculine sculptural streetscape, we hardly noticed, until on International Women's Day 2016 the feminist activist Caroline Criado Perez was jogging through the square and became incensed. Two years of campaigning later, the Suffragist Millicent Garrett Fawcett (1847–1929), sculpted by the distinguished sculptor Gillian Wearing (p. 136), was unveiled for the centenary of women getting the vote.

Born in Suffolk, the eighth of ten children, Millicent Garrett was, unusually for a nineteenth-century girl, sent to boarding school in London. With her went her older sister Elizabeth, later Elizabeth Garrett Anderson, Britain's first female doctor. Millicent began campaigning for women's suffrage at the age of 19, but this statue depicts her (like the men) as a mature, determined figure of authority. She's shown at 50, when she became president of the largest women's rights organisation, the National Union of Women's Suffrage Societies (NUWSS), which she led for 20 years.

Fawcett was extensively published, her writings including the introduction to a centenary edition of *A Vindication of the Rights of Woman* by Mary Wollstonecraft (p. 128), and in 1871 she co-founded Cambridge University's Newnham College for women. As a Suffragist, Fawcett made sure her

Millicent Fawcett addressing a Hyde Park rally around 1915.

campaigning was always legal and peaceful, in contrast to the more militant Suffragettes. They too are represented here, however: Fawcett's plinth carries 59 names of contributors to the cause, most accompanied by photos. Several are Suffragettes; four are men.

The banner Fawcett is holding quotes from a speech she made about the Suffragette Emily Wilding Davison, who died after stepping in front of the King's racehorse during the 1913 Derby. Fawcett thought this foolish, but her words, spoken years after the event, became a rallying cry. Unfortunately, despite adjustments designed to prevent this, the banner has gained the statue a nickname: 'Hanging out the washing'. It could only happen to a woman.

This remains the only free-standing female statue in Parliament Square, and the only one by a woman. The Suffragist does, however, stand under the watchful gaze of a raft of allegorical females on the façade of the Supreme Court.

An Interview with Gillian Wearing

How do you find seeing the statue in Parliament Square?

The nice surprise for me after the statue was installed was viewing it from behind; you see the silhouette of the banner Millicent carries and the Houses of Parliament, so there is this direct relation to the history and the lobbying Millicent had to do to get the vote through.

How did you get involved in the project?

I was approached along with other artists to submit an idea for a statue celebrating female suffrage in Parliament Square. I was so intrigued and flattered, and jumped at the chance.

Did you feel you were making history – out of history?

I didn't think of it like that, but it's a good way of putting it.

Do you feel particular pressure with this very public commission?

Not pressure, but it was different. Feminist campaigner Caroline Criado-Perez had noticed the lack of female presence in the square, and approached London Mayor Sadiq Khan to change this, so there was an allocated space and subject matter. I knew it was going to be visible for a long time, so it had to be just right. Everyone at City Hall was so supportive, and they are used to working with contemporary artists, so I didn't feel I was stepping into an entirely new world.

How did you approach Millicent Fawcett?

I read books about her, gathered images and worked with historians. Nothing changed in my perception of her; she had been overlooked for many years as she wasn't as newsworthy as the Suffragettes, but she was the actual person who got the first votes for women through.

Did you consciously draw on your 1992–3 project *Signs that say what you want them to say and*

*not signs that say what someone else wants you to
say* **when designing this statue with its banner?**
No, but there clearly are connections. To me
the banner was always pivotal, mainly because
Parliament Square is still a place for people to
meet for protests, and I wanted to reflect that.
It is recognition of the past and present.

**Does the 'Hanging out the Washing' moniker
irritate you?**
That comment came from a quickly made maquette
that was submitted for the initial Westminster
council meeting. I knew I was going to change
the way the banner was held. Millicent certainly
doesn't look like she is holding any washing now;
that's exactly how some people hold banners, and
banners were made of cloth in those days (as some
are today).

**How does your/her statue compare with the
statues of men in the square?**
As well as being the only statue proclaiming their
thoughts, this monument recognises the many
other women and men who supported and rallied
for female suffrage – including Suffragettes. Their
photographs are etched on tiles around the plinth
in chronological order of their birth. I think Fawcett
would have loved sharing that plinth with others.

Are you pleased with the statue?
When I walk past it, I am very proud. I love that it
now belongs in Parliament Square and has a life of
its own.

Nell Gwynn Stone, assumed 1937

Sculptor unknown; architect George Kay Green (1877–1939)

Nell Gwynn House, Sloane Avenue, SW3 3AX

Also: Venus Fountain, bronze, 1953, by Gilbert Ledward RA (1888–1960), Sloane Square, SW1W 8SB

High above the doorway of Nell Gwynn House, a mid-1930s Art Deco apartment block in Chelsea, stands 'Pretty, witty Nell', as her contemporary, the diarist Samuel Pepys, called her – though this rather pedestrian statue hardly does her justice.

Eleanor (Nell) Gwynn (1642/1650–87) was one of London's first actresses (most female parts having previously been played by young men). Women players were an innovation encouraged by Charles II on his restoration to the throne in 1660, when he enthusiastically reversed the Puritan Cromwellian ban on the theatre.

Women went from strength to strength as performers, but the stage remained inextricably linked with promiscuity and prostitution, not helped by Charles himself using it as a source of mistresses. Nell Gwynn was a famous royal favourite for more than 15 years, signalled here by the King Charles spaniel snuggled at her feet.

Gwynn's birth date is contested (as is the exact spelling of her surname), her early life unclear, though she probably grew up in poverty in Covent Garden, possibly in a brothel where her alcoholic mother worked. Gwynn's first theatre job was as a scantily clad 'orange-girl' selling fruit at the King's Playhouse (today's Theatre Royal, Drury Lane) and taking messages between men in the audience and actresses backstage. She graduated to acting around 1664 and Pepys praised her comic performances, but said serious roles 'she spoils'.

Like an actor, the statue has changed its make-up many times. 'I've seen it painted apricot, green

(terrible!) then stone colour,' says building manager Geoff Armes. 'In 2021 the gold was added.' A resident pointed out, he adds, that the statue looks less like the original Gwynn as seen in portraits than like Anna Neagle playing her in the 1934 film *Nell Gwynn*.

Royal favour gave Gwynn luxury and influence. She is said to have persuaded the king to found the nearby Royal Hospital, still home to the red-robed Chelsea Pensioners, and she would have travelled with Charles along the King's Road – built as a private route for the monarch to reach his palace at Kew.

Their relationship is celebrated again close by in

a watery relief on the Venus fountain in Sloane Square. Beneath an angular goddess of love, an elegant Gwynn fans herself as Charles picks fruit (an orange?) and Cupid fingers his arrows.

Gwynn had two sons by the King. The younger, James, died in childhood. The elder, Charles Beauclerk, became Duke of St Albans, and Gwynn's descendants are aristocrats to this day.

Sister Nivedita Painted bronze, 2023

By Nirjan De

Lake Rd, junction with Leopold Rd, Wimbledon, SW19 7HB

A little larger than life, this golden statue stands defiantly on a traffic island outside a girls' school in suburban Wimbledon. It looks rather out of place, but that isn't wholly inappropriate for the woman it commemorates – a lively and at times controversial writer, campaigner and educator, especially of women.

Margaret Noble (1867–1911) was raised a devout Methodist, and toyed with Catholicism before finding Church dogma unsatisfactory and studying natural science and Buddhism. Finally she became a disciple of a Hindu guru, who gave her the name

Sister Nivedita ('the dedicated'), and in 1898 led her to Kolkata (then Calcutta). There she did indeed become known for her dedication – to India, its people, its arts and science, and its self-determination.

Born in Dungannon, Northern Ireland,

Noble moved to Yorkshire and trained as a teacher, becoming interested in the then-new child-centred educational methods of Froebel, inventor of the kindergarten and proponent of play-based learning. Moving to Wimbledon in 1890, she founded progressive schools for girls here, joined London's intellectual circles (meeting the likes of Bernard Shaw, p. 172) and publicly supported Home Rule for Ireland. In 1895 she met the visiting Hindu monk, philosopher and inspirational interfaith preacher Narendranath Dutta or Guru Swami Vivekananda.

Dutta said later that he was seeking 'a real lioness to work for the Indians, women especially', and Noble fitted the bill. She joined his religious community

and, as Nivedita, founded a girls' school in Kolkata,
cared for the sick during an outbreak of plague
and wrote extensively and sympathetically about
local culture, including the role of women. Initially
a supporter of colonial rule, she soon became
disillusioned and, particularly horrified by the 1905
partition of Bengal (along religious lines), fiercely
championed Indian independence, even backing
groups using violence.

By the time she died in Darjeeling aged 42 she
was something of heroine in India, where schools
and colleges (and a bridge) are named after her
and a national postage stamp was issued for her
centenary. With a blue plaque already on her home
in Wimbledon, the UK Friends of Sister Nivedita
wanted a full-scale statue here. They commissioned
a traditional bronze figure from Calcutta, but
the casting in a backyard forge was faulty and –
without consultation – the foundry painted over
the cracks. London was somewhat surprised to
receive this golden effigy. But as Marcus Beale, the
architect who helped install it, says, 'It is a cultural
artefact plucked from Calcutta to Wimbledon, a
reinterpretation of this Irish woman who worked
for India…and the girls at the girls' school have
taken her up, which is perfect because girls'
education was her life's work.'

So Sister Nivedita stands in unconventional
cross-cultural gaudy glory on an unremarkable
suburban street – facing east.

Noor Inayat Khan Bronze, 2012

By Karen Newman (b. 1951)

North-east corner of Gordon Square Gardens, WC1H 0PY

See also: SOE Memorial (p. 200)

A formidable World War II spy who single-handedly kept communications open between London and the Paris Resistance after her comrades were captured by the Gestapo, Noor Inayat Khan (1914–44) is represented here by a face that looks less strong and determined than open, warm and kind. And it makes this memorial all the more moving.

Even the people who trained her for the SOE (Special Operations Executive) identified Khan's gentleness – sometimes with concern. Nonetheless, in 1943 she became the first female radio operator infiltrated into occupied France, a role that then came with a life expectancy of six weeks. Khan lasted a little longer, before being captured, tortured and shot at Dachau in 1944, aged just 30.

She put her life on the line not out of British patriotism but passionate anti-Fascism. She was determined to contribute to the war effort but did not want to kill. A British Indian Muslim with an American mother, she was born in Moscow and grew up in Paris and London. Her father's family were prominent Sufis and Indian nationalists. Her great-great-grandfather, Tipu Sultan, 'The Tiger of Mysore', died fighting the British.

Having studied music and child psychology in France, Khan (also known as Nora Baker, from her mother's maiden name) wrote poetry and children's books until the outbreak of war.

Noor Inayat Khan's brother with the George Cross posthumously awarded to his sister in 1949.

The family escaped Paris just before the German occupation, and in Britain Khan joined the WAAF before being recruited to the SOE (to which there is a collective memorial – p. 200). She was given the disguise of a children's nurse and codenamed Madeleine before being sent back across the Channel. After her death she was awarded the George Cross and the French Croix de Guerre.

For part of her childhood and throughout her wartime stay in London, Khan lived at 4 Taviton Street, just off Gordon Square, and enjoyed the gardens here, so this was a natural choice for her memorial. Following a campaign that raised £100,000, the bust was commissioned from London portrait sculptor Karen Newman, who worked for many years on waxworks at nearby Madame Tussauds. In 2012 the statue was unveiled by the Princess Royal.

Touchingly, little offerings – flowers, candles etc. – are still left here by admirers.

The Oceanides White Carrara marble, late nineteenth century

Seven a-little-more-than-life-size naked marble women hang out at the water's edge on rocks and overgrown shells, as if they've just emerged from a swim or are about to plunge in. Several look up apparently in admiration at an eighth, more idealised, woman who stands atop two dynamic winged horses.

Locals know them simply as 'the naked ladies', and one told me she remembers climbing on them as a schoolgirl in the 1970s when 'they all had graffiti in rude places'. Today they have been fully restored and are officially the Oceanides, water nymphs of Greek mythology. Their bodies are more human than most nineteenth-century legendary ladies, their hair wilder and faces livelier and more mischievous.

Originally commissioned from Italy for the Surrey estate of British financier Whittaker Wright, once known as the richest man in the world, they were never even unpacked, because in 1904 Wright was found guilty of fraud and took a cyanide pill in court. The statues were purchased for £600 by Indian businessman and philanthropist Sir Ratan Tata, who had just bought York House.

This Thameside Twickenham estate dates back to the fifteenth century, the house to the seventeenth, and it had many royal connections, British and

French, before Tata became its last private owner. He commissioned the Italianate gardens centred on the Oceanides, installed here in 1909. In the absence of any instructions for their composition, the layout was designed by landscape architects J. Cheal and Sons, and the artist's intentions are still debated. Some of the women originally held pearls (and one or two hands still look set to do so), and subjects including pearl fishers, Pegasus and the Birth of Venus have all been suggested.

The designation as Ancient Greek water nymphs, however, has stuck. Daughters of the earth-encircling River God Oceanus and sea goddess Tethys, the 'three thousand' Oceanides (or Oceanids) brought life-giving freshwater springs and rain to nature and humanity, as well as being handmaidens of Artemis (see also p. 35) and wives, lovers, nursemaids and mothers to many key figures in Greek mythology. Their children include the Graces or Charities (p. 186), Prometheus, Atlas, Circe and Nike (p. 194), and they were charged with the protection of youths.

There is certainly a youthful playfulness about this installation and, given its mysterious origins, you can interpret it as you will.

Mother and Child

Mother and Child sculptures cut across time and geography, near-universal symbols of love and the continuity of human life. London has quite a range. There are Madonna and Child statues, of course (p. 108) and personifications of Charity as a breastfeeding mother (p. 34 and p. 165), but there are also more down-to-earth examples . . .

This touching mother-and-child bust was commissioned by the charity at the nearby Great Ormond Street Hospital for Children, and was close to the sculptor's heart. Having trained as a doctor, Patricia Finch married a fellow student, and took her finals pregnant with their first child Helen (later the model for *Golders Hill Girl*, p. 74). She failed, so she became 'an old-fashioned GP's wife', says her second daughter, Lucie Skeaping – and, using her anatomical knowledge, a portrait sculptor.

This commission – modelled on the wife and child of one of Great Ormond Street's male doctors – was one of Finch's last, and it was special. 'I was in Great Ormond Street when I was one,' says Skeaping. 'I nearly died, and my mother never forgot it. Each Christmas she took me to the hospital to give the children presents.' When Finch herself died, her daughters found resin copies of several of her works,

Mother and Child among them. 'Most went to the Oxfam shop,' says Skeaping, 'but I kept this one and it's in my garden. It looks even better part-covered in ivy.'

With faces on both sides – looking towards the main entrance of the hospital and away – this mother is clothed in nature – carved with leaves and vegetation. The figures were donated to the hospital by a local sculptor known as the 'penniless philanthropist'. A trained actor, self-taught sculptor and recovered addict who has twice (yes, twice) rescued people intent on suicide from the tracks of London Underground, he gives rather than sells his art. Another of his sculptures, *Angel of the Finchley Memorial* (oak and stainless steel), stands outside the children's cancer ward.

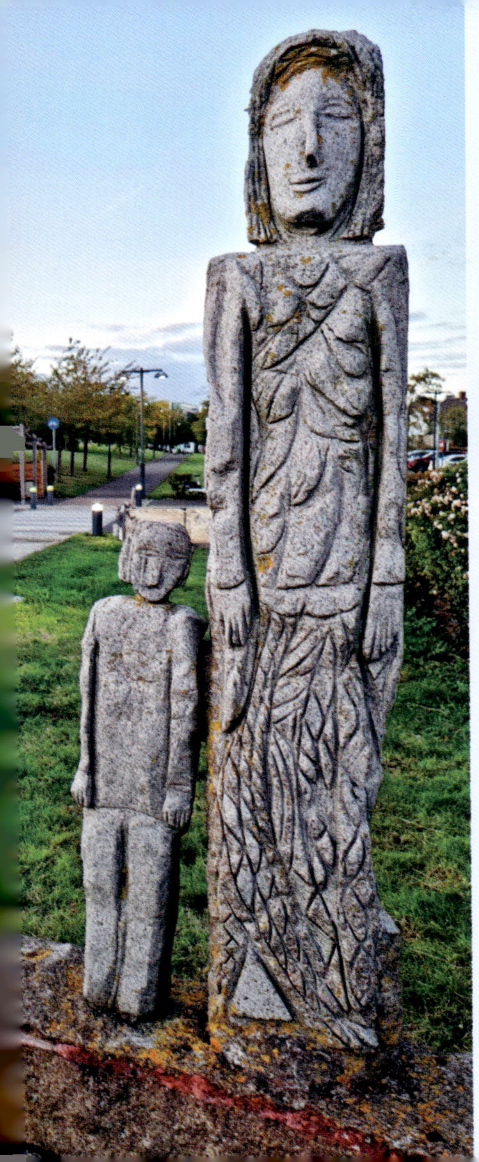

Protection

Affection

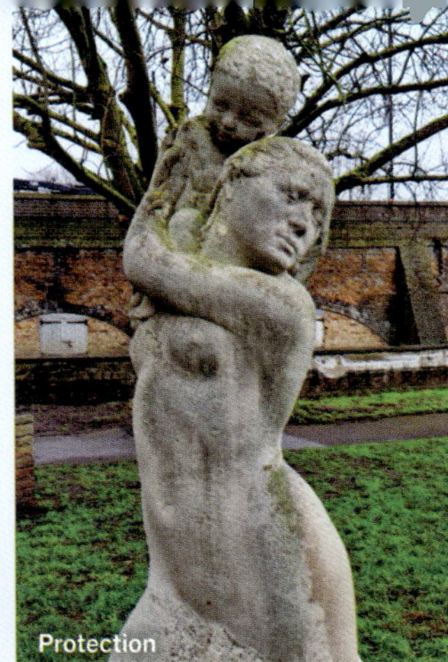

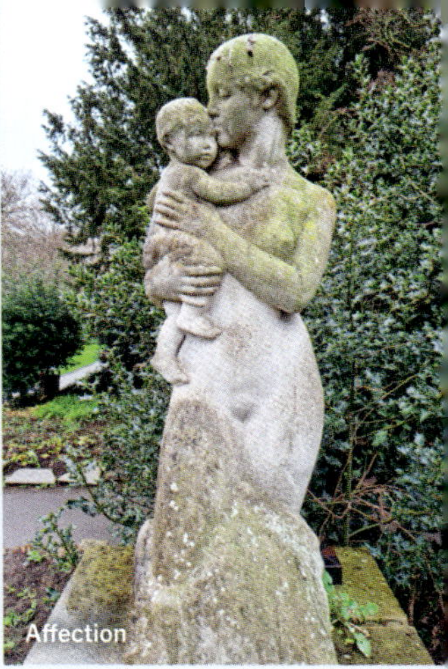

Protection (mother and child), with *Adoration, Grief and Leda*. Installed here 1953. Stone, 1940s: Four sculptures by James Wedgewood (1886–1973).
Affection by Joseph Hermon Cawthra. Stone, 1963.

Pryor's Bank, Bishop's Park, by Putney Bridge (North end), SW6 3LA.

Two mother and child statues are among five emotionally charged sculptures – all featuring women – in this little Thames-side public garden. *Affection* evokes exactly that while unusually combining motherhood with a gentle eroticism. Made two decades earlier, *Protection* looks in some ways more modern: the mother's body turned, holding the child aloft out of harm's way. She emerges from a rocky base with just a little less of her lower body visible than *Affection*'s, and the mother's love, as befits the title, more defensive. Evocative too are *Adoration*, a naked couple, and *Grief*, a young couple clinging to one another, heartbreakingly slumped over their lifeless child.

Prudence – Prudentia

1. Above the main entrance to Holborn Bars ('Prudential Assurance building'), now archway to Waterhouse Square, 138–42 Holborn, EC1N 2SW.
Terracotta, 1898. Architect, Alfred Waterhouse; sculptor, William Birnie Rhind (1853–1933).

2. Lewisham High Street, corner of Limes Grove ('Prudential Buildings'), SE13 6AA.
Terracotta, 1908. By Frederick William Pomeroy (1856–1924).

3. Prudence, Justice and Liberality Norwich Union Building, 49–50 Fleet Street, EC4A 2EA.
Portland stone, 1913. By Arthur Stanley Young.
See also (and for image) p. 93.

4. Confidence, Prudence, Justice, Truth, Thrift and Self-Denial. Metropolitan Life Assurance Building, 13 Moorgate, EC2R 6AD.
Stone, 1890–3. Architect, Aston Webb; sculptor, William Silver Frith.

In the nineteenth century Prudence was adopted by insurance companies as the ideal front woman for their brands, and all four of these statues were created in this context.

Prudentia, or simply Prudence, is the personification of one of the four Cardinal Virtues first described by Ancient Greek philosophers (the others being Fortitude, Temperance, p. 32, and Justice, p. 90). Prudence represents sound judgement, and was regarded as the foundation or mother virtue, since without her the others will not be well used.

Looking prominently down on Holborn is Prudentia of the Prudential Assurance Company, insurers to one-third of the UK population at the time

of her creation. She had represented the business since its inception in 1848, when its founders stated their aim as to 'infix habits of prudence', and based their logo on a painting of the Virtue by Sir Joshua Reynolds.

Prudentia stands here above the entrance to 'the Pru's' striking late-Victorian headquarters, statement architecture in red granite, red brick and red terracotta (by the designer of the Natural History Museum). A state-of-the-art office, it had some supremely paternalistic Victorian provision: 'Lady Clerks' were given their own entrance, staircase, library, roof terrace and dining room, and were allowed to leave work 15 minutes early so they were not obliged to mix with the men.

Prudentia, her robes slightly off the shoulder and elegantly trimmed, holds a hand mirror for self-reflection. She appears again on the Lewisham branch

of 'the Pru', also in red terracotta, but with a more sedate, reliable vibe. Simply and fully robed, she looks demurely down and holds symbols of wisdom: a book and a serpent (snake).

Prudence often accompanies Justice (as one might hope), and they are seen together on City façades built for the Norwich Union (Fleet Street, p. 93) and Metropolitan Life Assurance (Moorgate, p. 92). Norwich Union's motto was *'Prudens Simplicitas'* (Prudent Simplicity, pictured p. 92), and here Prudence sits in an aesthetically pleasing (and not particularly simple) sculptural group, with blindfold Justice and a cherubic Liberality pouring coins and fruit from a cornucopia. 'We may suppose that Prudence has a premium ledger somewhere about her', an employee who liked the image nonetheless commented at the time, 'otherwise the sculpture does not represent the business.'

At Moorgate she stands in a group of six Victorian virtues arrayed across the corner tower, appropriately placed between Confidence and Justice.

Queen Alexandra

Royal London Hospital (opposite the Stepney Way entrance), Whitechapel, E1 2JH.
Bronze, 1908: By George Edward Wade (1853–1933)

Queen Alexandra Memorial, Marlborough Rd (opposite St James's Palace), SW1A 1BQ
Bronze, 1932: By Alfred Gilbert (1854–1934)

Victoria & Albert Museum façade, Cromwell Rd, SW7 2RL
Portland stone, 1909: By By architect Aston Webb and sculptor William Goscombe John.

See p. 148, 165, 168.

Elegant and poised, in stylishly regal robes and raised on a stone pedestal, Queen Alexandra looks a little

incongruous against the modern glass-and-steel Royal London Hospital. The old hospital (from which she was moved), however, had close connections with this 'people's princess' and popular queen, wife of Edward VII.

Born into a minor branch of the Danish royal family, Alexandra (1844–1925) grew up in relatively modest and informal circumstances, sharing a room with her sister Dagmar (later Empress of Russia), making her own clothes, ice skating, riding, taking lessons from women's swimming pioneer Nancy Edberg and serving at the family table – as well as occasionally enjoying visits from storyteller Hans Christian Anderson.

The family's status (but not finances) changed in 1852 when a succession crisis resulted in Alexandra's

father being named heir to the Danish throne. In 1863 he became Christian IX, Alexandra's brother was elected George I of Greece and she, aged 18, married Edward Prince of Wales, heir to Queen Victoria (p. 164).

Her relationship with her husband was mostly cordial despite his philandering. Her mother-in-law was trickier, especially when Victoria backed Prussia (where her daughter was married to the Imperial heir) in its invasion of Denmark. All Alexandra's six (much-loved) children were 'born premature', and her biographer Richard Hough suggests she adjusted her due dates to avoid Victoria attending.

Even Victoria, however, valued the public's love of this attractive, vivacious, hard-working and unstuffy

woman who spent a record 39 years as Princess of Wales. Denied political influence, she devoted herself to charitable work, especially women's welfare and hospitals, particularly the London (only 'Royal' since 1990). It was from here that the surgeon Sir Frederick Treves came to Edward's rescue when he got appendicitis just before his 1901 coronation. The ceremony was delayed but the prince survived to become king – and make Alexandra queen.

President of the London Hospital from 1904, she visited patients regularly (including the famous Elephant Man), empathising through her own disability – a limp caused by rheumatic fever. She introduced from Denmark an ultra-violet light treatment for dermal tuberculosis (lupus), and Britain's first Finsen lamp can be seen in use on this statue's base.

The queen also appears along with her husband and Victoria on the façade of the V&A, which was started in Victoria's reign but completed in Edward and Alexandra's.

After Alexandra died, a memorial was placed on the garden wall of Marlborough House, Alexandra and Edward's London home until he came to the throne, and hers after he died. It was unveiled by her son

George V to the accompaniment of music composed for the occasion by Edward Elgar.

The sculptor explained that the memorial showed 'Love Enthroned' supported by Faith and Hope sending a boy out across the 'River of Life'. Allegorical as this statue may be, it would be easy to mistake Love Enthroned for Alexandra – which is perhaps not accidental.

Queen Anne

In front of St Paul's Cathedral, copy
Sicilian marble (1886, by Richard Claude Belt and Louis-Auguste Malempré) of 1709–12 original commissioned by Christopher Wren, sculpted by Francis Bird (1667–1731)

Market Square House, Kingston-upon-Thames, KT1 1JS.
Gilded metal, 1706. By Francis Bird

Outside 13 Queen Anne's Gate, SW1H 9BU.
Stone, 1705: Sculptor uncertain, possibly also by Francis Bird. Stone, (by 1708), probably moved a little way to its present position c.1810, repairs by John Thomas 1862.

See also: Clusters of Queens (p. 158), Britannia (p. 42)

Queen Anne (1665–1714) stands imperiously in front of St Paul's Cathedral, the royal sceptre wand-like in her hand. She could have done with some magic. Plagued by ill health, she endured 17 pregnancies that produced just five live babies. Only one survived infancy, and he tragically succumbed to smallpox aged 11.

The younger daughter of James, Duke of York (later James II of England/VII of Scotland), Anne was six when her mother died. Separated from her Catholic father, she was raised Protestant under the protection/control of her uncle Charles II. In 1688, with her father now king, Anglican Anne supported his deposition by her sister Mary and her Dutch Protestant husband, William of Orange.

The new joint monarchs did not, however, approve of the shy Anne's intense relationship with Lady Sarah Churchill, who wielded increasing influence over her. The resulting rift was only mended after Mary died childless (also of smallpox), leaving Anne as William's heir.

Anne came to the throne in 1702, weeks after the opening of Sir Christopher Wren's St Paul's, and the Queen's statue here had her full approval. There was in fact a plan to build 50 new Anglican churches, each with a statue of Anne. Only the first of these figures was made – for St Mary le Strand (WC2R 1ES) – and it was never erected at the church.

Instead, it was placed on an elegant, newly built terrace in Westminster, where local children were soon pelting it, believing it to be Catholic Queen Mary, causing serious damage. It was repaired in the nineteenth century, and identification added, but the damage continued, and the statue remains ill-maintained compared with the ultra-desirable Queen Anne houses around it.

Less mistreated, though almost as unnoticed, Anne

also stands in golden dominion over the marketplace of Kingston-upon-Thames. Sparklingly garbed, the effigy was commissioned by a local alderman from the same sculptor who went on to do the work for St Paul's.

This fared less well. Unveiled as the Peace of Utrecht was signed, ending the War of the Spanish Succession, the Queen's statue suffered attacks, some reportedly fomented by the Whig opposition. A popular rhyme (in various versions) soon spread:

Brandy-faced Nan
Left in the lurch
Face to the gin-shop
Back to the church.

There was a gin palace on Ludgate Hill (which she faces), and Anne did enjoy a tipple, but the ditty is unfair to a diligent monarch. She oversaw the Act of Union (1707) which created the United Kingdom, and advanced the cause of a constitutional monarchy by working with Parliament.

Her St Paul's effigy is surrounded by four female personifications of her realm: Britania (with trident,

see also p. 42), France (helmeted), Ireland (with harp) and America (a semi-naked caricature Native American). By the 1880s vandalism had left it so damaged that the statue was quietly removed (to be found a few years later, deserted in a stonemason's yard and reconstructed at private Holmhurst House near Hastings). A replacement copy was unveiled in Queen Victoria's Jubilee year.

The maker of the copy, Richard Claude Belt, was a controversial figure. Known as 'the charlatan sculptor' following an infamous libel case against a fellow artist (which he won in court but not in the art world), he was soon imprisoned for fraud, and Louis-Auguste Malempré finished the job.

Criticism continued, and in 1897 Queen Victoria (p. 164) was asked for permission to remove the statue. 'Move Queen Anne?' she apparently replied. 'Certainly not! Why, it might someday be suggested that my statue should be removed, which I should much dislike.'

Queen Charlotte Lead, 1775

Sculptor unknown

North end of Queen Square Gardens, Bloomsbury, WC1N 3AR

Also of note: in Queen Square is Sam (the Cat), a memorial to Patricia Penn, a local nurse, activist and cat lover who in 1971 campaigned to save Queen Charlotte's Hospital.

'Widely regarded' as representing Queen Charlotte (1744–1818) – according to the plaque beneath the statue – the queen stands in royal regalia, looking benignly down at us, and across the gardens towards a touching twentieth-century sculpture of a mother and child (p. 146). All this is highly appropriate to Queen Charlotte, who was reportedly good-natured

and informal (for a queen), a keen botanist who vastly expanded Kew Gardens, and an invaluable patron of the nearby maternity hospital (now called Queen Charlotte's) – as well as the loving mother of 15 children, and our longest serving

Queen Consort, wife of George III.

On 8 September 1761, 17-year-old German princess Charlotte of Mecklenburg Strelitz arrived in London. It was quite a day. She met her husband-to-be for the first time, changed into her diamond-encrusted wedding dress (which nearly fell off because she'd lost so much weight being sea-sick on the voyage) and was married to the 22-year-old King – all within six hours.

The match nonetheless proved successful – at least for the first quarter-century. Then the King's mental health deteriorated, distressing and terrifying his queen and perplexing his (mostly incompetent) doctors. The nation was left with 'Mad King George' and a Prince Regent. Charlotte's son ruled, but she retained custody of the King, often accompanying him to the calm of Kew. But she saw less and less of him as he became more unpredictable and violent, and she became sadder and more irritable. Her mood was not helped by the plight of her long-time penfriend Marie Antoinette in the French Revolution.

This statue was erected in happier times, when the royal couple were known for their genial patronage of contemporary musicians – especially Handel. An eight-year-old Mozart played for them at Buckingham House (now Palace), the home the King had just bought for the Queen, the young prodigy apparently accompanying her as she sang.

Charlotte has had a low profile in modern times – at least until *Bridgerton* hit our screens. The show's depiction of her as black was not entirely a modern invention; rumours of African blood circulated even in her lifetime, in part due to a physician describing her as having 'a true mulatto face'. The chances that she was actually a woman of colour are minuscule, but this statue, with its slightly flared nose and unusual casting in dark lead, will serve history and *Bridgerton* fans alike.

That is as long as we accept that this is Queen Charlotte. The statue's genesis is unclear, and in the nineteenth century it was assumed to be Queen Anne, after whom Queen Square is named. The English Heritage historian Steven Brindle is convinced it is Anne, 'because of the hair'. This is indeed strikingly similar to Anne's other statues (see p. 152), but we have no clearly identified statues of Queen Charlotte to compare with, and Anne's nose is usually narrow, which the Queen Square queen's is not. You decide!

Queen Elizabeth I Stone (and paint), made for Ludgate 1586 or 1670–99

'Good Queen Bess', 'the Virgin Queen', 'Gloriana' . . . Elizabeth I (1533–1603) has a special place in English history and imagination – and in the story of statues of women in London. The St Dunstan's effigy of her is the capital's oldest public statue of a real woman – possibly of any individual (see p. 222).

Like the Queen herself, whose father beheaded her mother, whose half-sister imprisoned her, and who reigned solo for 45 years in a man's world, the statue has suffered and endured.

Created for nearby Ludgate (one of the original gates through London Wall), either at its Elizabethan renovation in 1586 (which would make this the only surviving statue carved in the Queen's lifetime) or for its post-Great Fire reconstruction (1670–99), this Elizabeth certainly stood on the west side of Ludgate until its demolition in 1760 to allow London's expansion. The statue was moved to the medieval church of St Dunstan-in-the-West, only for this too to be demolished in 1829 to make way for more traffic.

Elizabeth was then 'lost' until 1839, when workmen demolishing (yes, again) a local pub found the statue forgotten in the basement. It was re-erected in its present position on the new St Dunstan's (built 1831–3). In 1928 Elizabeth was taken down once more, but this time to be cleaned, restored, repainted and returned to her niche. She was (re)unveiled by the Suffragist Millicent Fawcett (p. 134) in the same month women finally got the equal right to vote. Clearly an Elizabeth devotee, Fawcett left £70 in her will for the upkeep of the statue.

Harrow, originally at Ashridge Park.

Sadly this 'private income' was insufficient to keep the Queen in the manner to which she should have been accustomed. Today she looks imperiously down from above the vestry door, her gown gloriously patterned, her cloak ermine-trimmed, but her appearance unquestionably faded. Nearly a century after Fawcett, the church is trying to raise funds to again bring Gloriana back to glory.

The daughter of Henry VIII and Anne Boleyn, Queen Bess did much: stabilised England, established the Anglican Church, encouraged the arts (including Shakespeare), defeated the Spanish Armada and founded several schools, including Westminster (1560) and Harrow (1572). In public statuary, Westminster has repaid her poorly, with a dire depiction atop a school war memorial (p. 171). Harrow does her better, with a suitably regal full-length effigy sporting a golden crown, orb and sceptre, though she peers down on their tail-coated pupils with a look of stern disapproval.

Clusters of Queens

Kimpton Fitzroy Hotel.

Two quartets and a trio of queens cluster on the exteriors of buildings in central London. In each case the same three queens form the core – Victoria, Elizabeth I and Anne (see also, respectively, p. 164, p. 156 and p. 152).

Victoria was on the throne when all three clusters were created, and the earlier queens seem to be a kind of backing group for the monarch – a validation of female rule. Elizabeth I is an obvious candidate, having seen off the Spanish, established the Church of England and lasted 45 years on the throne. Anne, despite a pre-coronation image of weakness, was an engaged and effective monarch who ruled for 12 years with no help from her beloved but ineffectual husband, and brought the home nations together into the United Kingdom.

At Hotel Russell (as it was when it opened in 1900), the life-size statues are surprisingly generic, given that they were made by a leading sculptor of the day. Here

Maughan Library.

the trio is joined by Mary II (1662–94). Anne's older sister, she co-ruled with her husband William of Orange after dethroning her father, Catholic James II (with Anglican Anne's approval) – so there's perhaps an additional theme here of female defenders of the Church of England.

The fourth queen on the Maughan Library, on the other hand, is Matilda (1102–67), never actually crowned queen but certainly a royal force to be reckoned with. Daughter of King Henry I, she was married aged 11 to Henry V of Germany, soon Holy Roman Emperor, and by her mid-teens was Regent of Italy. Henry died in 1125, and Matilda returned to her father's realm and was pushed into a political marriage (aged 26) to the 14-year-old Geoffrey of Anjou.

Matilda's only legitimate brother having died in the *White Ship* disaster, Henry I named Matilda his heir – and made the barons swear to honour this. When Henry died in 1135, however, the barons put Matilda's (male) cousin Stephen of Blois on the throne, and so began the Anarchy, nearly two decades of Stephen and Matilda fighting for the crown. Matilda was de facto queen for several years, and finally in 1153 the Treaty of Wallingford named her son heir to Stephen. In 1154 he became Henry II, and his mother a royal adviser with her own court in Normandy.

What of the queens left out of the clusters? By Victoria's reign there had been only two others since 1066. Mary Tudor was a legitimate queen, but she was also Catholic, not an appropriate advocate for Victoria as head of the Church of England. And Lady Jane Grey, though intelligent, was manipulated into queenhood aged 17 and lasted just nine days before Mary Tudor took the throne and had her executed – hardly a model of female monarchy any good Victorian would wish to promote.

Guildhall.

Queen Elizabeth II Bronze, 2023

Our longest reigning monarch, more than 70 years on the throne, Queen Elizabeth II (1926–2022) amazingly has only one public statue in London – and that only unveiled in 2023, a year after her death. This is in sharp contrast to our second-longest-serving monarch, Elizabeth's great-great grandmother, Queen Victoria (p. 164), the most memorialised person in Britain, whose consort Prince Albert commissioned this building which she opened in 1871.

Elizabeth and her husband Prince Philip, Duke of Edinburgh, flank the south entrance to this popular concert venue. Life-like figures in civilian evening dress, they seem to be just stepping out of their niches to go into the hall. In life, they came here many times. Elizabeth attended her first Albert Hall performance in 1934 aged eight and her last – her hundred-and-thirtieth – just pre-pandemic in 2019.

These dynamic statues of queen and consort echo and contrast with those of Victoria and Albert which stand either side of the north entrance. Part of the same 2021 hundred-and-fiftieth anniversary project to fill the hall's last empty niches, the latter are more traditional, pure white figures. Static, they nonetheless gesture towards the doorway, welcoming us in.

Back on the south side, Philip looks across at the Queen, while she is turned towards us. The young sculptor, Poppy Field, who won the commission in a year-long competition, has said she wanted to depict their enduring love story as well as royalty. Field usually

works from life in long face-face sittings but this time, though beginning before the Queen's death, she had no access to her subjects. She was restricted to information publicly available, and dressed up models Megan and Jack to get verisimilitude and the sense of the royal couple 'leading us into the hall'.

The Queen's musical taste was apparently more *Showboat* than Stockhausen, but she championed all kinds of music throughout her reign. In 2005 she introduced the Queen's Medal for Music, and in 2014 appointed the first woman, Judith Weir (b. 1954), to the ancient role of Master of the Queen's Music. Elizabeth's son, King Charles III, is a known classical music lover and has taken over the late queen's role as patron of the Royal Albert Hall. On Remembrance Day 2023 he unveiled his mother's first, and so far only, London statue.

Queen Elizabeth the Queen Mother Bronze, 2009

By Philip Jackson (b. 1944). With a 1955 bronze of Edward VI by William McMillan (1887–1977) and two bronze reliefs of the Queen's life by Paul Day (b. 1967)

The Mall (bottom of steps to Carlton Gardens), SW1Y 5AA

Queen Elizabeth, the Queen Mother (1900–2002), stands robust and smiling beneath a flamboyantly feathered hat, part of her Order of the Garter robes. Behind her, her husband King George VI looks more uncertain. So it was in life. He never wanted or expected to be king, but was thrust onto the throne when his older brother Edward VIII abdicated in 1937 to marry American divorcée Wallis Simpson. George had a stammer, creating a vicious circle of nervousness in public, and his wife supported him throughout his reign, especially during the Second World War.

Her statue was funded by the sale of a £5 coin celebrating the eightieth birthday of her daughter Queen Elizabeth II, and the Queen Mother is shown aged 51, at the time she was widowed. Living another half century, this ever-popular royal attended public engagements until a few months before her death at 101.

Born Elizabeth Bowes-Lyon, probably in London, the ninth of ten children of two English aristocrats, she was better educated than most 'ladies' of the time. While four older brothers fought in the First World War and one died, she spent her teens helping run a convalescent home for wounded soldiers at her parents' 650-year-old Scottish ancestral seat, Glamis Castle (said to have inspired Shakespeare's *Macbeth*).

Reluctant to accept the limitations of royal life, Elizabeth twice turned down proposals of marriage from 'Bertie', Prince Albert (George was his regnal

HM The Queen Mother, bronze bust by Oscar Nemon, 1979, Grocers' Company Courtyard, Princes St, EC2R 8AD
Presented to the Grocers' Company by its liverymen to mark the eight-hundredth anniversary of the first mention of the company, this joyous bust of the Queen Mother reflects her reputation for conviviality, and was approved and unveiled in 1980 by the lady herself, who had been First Lady Honorary Freeman of the Company since 1953.

The Queen Mother during her hundredth-birthday celebrations.

name), before they were finally married in Westminster Abbey in 1923. Known for connecting with people of all classes, nationalities and ethnicities (except, having lived through the horrors of both world wars, the Germans), she was a great asset to the royal family.

Lively reliefs flank her statue showing her enjoying two of her favourite things - horse racing and corgis - and in a domestic setting with her husband and daughters. We also see her on a bombed street talking to Londoners, as she did during the war. The royal couple stayed in the capital throughout the Blitz, and when Buckingham Palace took several hits, the Queen famously said, 'I'm glad we've been bombed. It makes me feel I can look the East End in the face.'

Now she smiles congenially down on everyone – locals, tourists and today's royal family – as they pass along the Mall, London's red-carpet road, between Trafalgar Square and Buckingham Palace.

Queen Victoria 14 statues (and see also Clusters of Queens, p. 158)

There are more statues in London of Queen Victoria (1819–1901) than of any other woman – more, in fact, than of any other person. And not just in London, but the whole country. It is possible that she is the most memorialised woman in the world. But let's get back to London, which was Victoria's primary home throughout her life . . .

Victoria was born in London's Kensington Palace, and lived here with her controlling mother until she was 18, when her uncle died and she became queen. Outside the palace, a youthful white marble Victoria wearing coronation robes looks out over Kensington Gardens.

Victoria herself attended the statue's inauguration in 1893, writing in her journal, 'It is a great pleasure to me to be here . . . in my dear old home, to witness the unveiling of this fine statue so admirably designed & executed by my beloved Daughter.'

The sculptor was Princess Louise, sixth of Victoria's nine children. The queen didn't much like babies, but they were the price of sex with her adored Prince Albert, which – never a Victorian prude – she makes clear in her writings she very much enjoyed. Louise sculpted this statue in her studio in Kensington Palace. Often called a feminist, the princess studied sculpture privately and at art school, and became an active patron of girls' education. After her husband died in 1914, she lived for 35 years in the palace behind her statue of her mother.

The teenage queen is portrayed again in a much more recent statue, commissioned by the residents of charming little Victoria Square, built just after the queen came to the throne. The statue states (in Latin) that it is 'Queen Victoria at the start of her victorious reign', and the sculptor, Catherine Anne Laugel, says she wanted to show her 'as a young woman first' and as a young queen second.

Laugel aimed to capture Victoria as she was described

in her early teens by the aristocratic artist Lady Wharncliffe, who said she had 'a nice countenance and distingué figure . . . born a princess without the least appearance of art or affectation'. Attired in a dress rather than royal regalia, she holds a simple rose, symbol of England, as if she has just picked it in the garden.

On becoming queen in 1837, Victoria moved to Buckingham Palace (and banished her mother to a separate apartment). Here we find her again enthroned in front of her palace home – but this is a very different Victoria. Commissioned by King Edward VII immediately after his mother's death, it came to be nicknamed 'the Wedding Cake'. So complex was this huge memorial that, with the accompanying redesign of its surroundings, it was a decade before it was finally unveiled a year after Edward's own death by his son (Victoria's grandson) George V.

A vast seated Victoria stares along the Mall. She seems imperious and stern – until you get closer, when she morphs into quite an ordinary-looking down-in-the-mouth, dumpy middle-aged woman. This is surely one of the statues Bernard Shaw had most in mind when he complained about London's unflattering effigies of the queen (see p. 172).

Victoria's life was of course anything but ordinary. She was queen of the UK, Empress of India and head of an empire covering almost a quarter of the globe.

And at the start of the twentieth century, statuary was a key way of making sure everyone knew it. Many parts of the empire contributed to funding this monument – even African tribes sent goods to be sold in its aid – and the Queen is surrounded here by a cornucopia of symbols representing empire and her presumed virtues (among them several under-dressed women – see also p. 100).

A golden-winged Victory (or Roman goddess Victoria) tops the composition, above gilded female personifications of Courage and Constancy. Behind the Queen, facing Buckingham Palace, is a charming if sentimental representation of Motherhood/Charity, for once legitimately bare-breasted as she feeds a baby. To the sides are angelic female figures of Truth (holding a mirror) and Justice (more on p. 90), clutching the arm of a suffering girl, while the lower levels are all about power: at sea (ship's prows, mermaids) and on land (bronze lions with symbolic men and women).

The Sculptor of the Buckingham Palace memorial statue, Sir Thomas Brock, had portrayed Queen Victoria before. His full-length statue of her in royal robes now stands alone under the portico of 15 Carlton House Terrace, as if pausing to pose after emerging from one of the street's elegant Nash houses (*c*.1830). It was commissioned in 1897 for the Queen's Diamond Jubilee by the Tory Constitutional Club.

When the club's building was demolished around 1959, the statue fell into private hands in Wimbledon, before being bought by the government in 1971 and installed here at what was then an outpost of the National Portrait Gallery. The house is now privately owned, but the statue remains part of the NPG's collection. The Queen looks slightly incongruous, but she adds another woman – joining nearby Florence Nightingale (p. 66) and Elizabeth, the Queen Mother (p. 162) – to an area thick with statues of 'heroic' men.

The Buckingham Palace memorial remains the largest to any individual in the UK besides the Albert Memorial,

which Victoria commissioned in memory of her husband after he died suddenly of typhoid in 1861 aged just 42. The Queen, also 42, never really recovered, and dressed in mourning black for the rest of her life, helping to create her dour image.

Albert's memorial stands in Kensington Gardens, directly opposite the Royal Albert Hall, the concert venue he founded, which Victoria opened ten years after his death. On its façade is a recent pure-white statue of her in happier times, paired with one of her beloved husband. Commissioned to mark the hall's hundred-and-fiftieth anniversary, they face each other across the north – originally main – entrance, open-handed, welcoming the public in.

Victoria proposed to her cousin Albert in 1839 (nobody proposes to a queen), and they married in 1840, the first wedding of a reigning monarch since Mary Tudor in 1554. Albert quickly became indispensable to the Queen in every aspect of her life, and his Great Exhibition of 1851 – also opened by Victoria – reshaped this area of London.

Before his death, Albert was involved in creating a memorial to this momentous event, with his Queen centre stage (surrounded by female figures representing Europe, America, Asia and Africa). After his death, however, she insisted the monument's main statue should be of him (more on this below). The Great Exhibition Memorial now stands opposite the south entrance to the Albert Hall, which is flanked by figures of Victoria's great-great grand-daughter Queen Elizabeth II and her consort Prince Philip (see p. 160).

A female personification of Peace, standing 3.3m tall atop 200 tonnes of Devon granite in this local park, has recently been re-identified as Queen Victoria as Peace. She is shown here just before Albert's death and her descent into mourning, and the figure was originally made for the Great Exhibition Memorial (see above). It was approved for the purpose by Prince Albert, but when he unexpectedly died, Victoria replaced herself on the monument with him. This 'spare' Victoria was displayed in South Kensington in 1862 and stood at

the Royal Horticultural Society until the site closed in 1888, when it disappears from the record.

In 1910, philanthropist Sydney Simmons donated Friary Park to the public with a grand opening

planned for 7 May. On the 6th, however, King Edward VII died. The ceremony was postponed (though the park opened), and a year later Simmons unveiled a memorial to the 'Peacemaker' king, known for restoring good relations with Europe, particularly through the 1904 Entente Cordiale with France. It isn't clear whether Simmons was unaware that the statue was actually of the King's mother, or whether, given its rather desultory treatment in the previous decade, he was asked (or chose) to keep this quiet.

Certainly, once in Friary Park, the statue was known for a century simply as Peace. That was until local historian Nick McKie started digging. He eventually unearthed the statue's true identity. In a 2022 restoration the spear the Queen had picked up somewhere on her journey was replaced with a replica of her original rod topped with a dove of peace.

The 1851 Great Exhibition showcased British and global innovation and industry. Attracting six million visitors in six months, it turned a hefty profit,

which contributed to the development of the South Kensington Museums – Science, Natural History and the Victoria and Albert (V&A). Queen Victoria tops the main entrance to the V&A with Albert just beneath her. By the time the museum opened, her son Edward VII was on the throne with Queen Alexandra (see also p. 150), so they also appear either side of the main entrance. Queen Alexandra is particularly recognisable (though binoculars or a zoom lens will help).

The Victorians (and Edwardians) didn't do things by halves; this is one impressive façade. Designed by Sir Aston Webb, who also re-designed Buckingham Palace, it is full of high-quality effigies. There are 32 individual full-length statues (by 21 sculptors) of important artists and architects – all helpfully named, all men. The only women are allegorical personifications of the men's skills, and the two queens.

Round the corner from the V&A, and also a beneficiary of Albert's exhibition, Imperial College boasts mascot lions called Vicky and Al and has its own regal statue

of Victoria. Just inside the college's twenty-first-century steel-and-glass atrium (public) – and visible through the window – stands a traditional full-length nineteenth-century marble Victoria, looking rather out of place. Her creator, J. E. Boehm, a prolific maker of public effigies, was Sculptor-in-Ordinary to the Queen from 1881 and taught sculpture to Princess Louise (see above), amid rumours of an affair.

This statue was commissioned by the University of London for Victoria's 1887 Golden Jubilee. From 1930 it was passed around – losing its crown along the way – before being officially (re)unveiled here in 2007 by Queen Elizabeth II.

Another Boehm Victoria stands in the middle of Fleet Street, rather distressed by traffic and weather. Her

dress, though, is delightfully decorated and her crown intact. Part of the Temple Bar Memorial, the queen is back to back with her son Prince Edward (later Edward VII), each flanked by columns carrying a potpourri of Victorian symbolism – hers referencing science and the arts, his war and peace. All this is crammed onto a narrow monument. It had to be narrow as the memorial replaced the Temple Bar gateway into the City (the one used by royalty), which was removed to improve traffic flow.

There was a full-scale, social-media-worthy brouhaha about this memorial and its cost. Much of the ire was directed at the chunky bronze 'griffin' atop the monument – in fact a dragon, the traditional protector of the City – and at the monument's unveiling the crowd actually booed.

It nonetheless carries three rather wonderful reliefs along with the statues. Two show Queen Victoria at this spot, probably on her first and last passages through Temple Bar. We see her in progress to Guildhall soon after her accession in 1837, and in a lavish 1872 procession to St Paul's with Prince Edward to give thanks for his recovery from typhoid (which had killed his father). The third relief shows Time (male) and Fortune (female) drawing a curtain over the old Temple Bar. Here the gate is shown in miniature, complete with its statues including a tiny effigy of another queen, Anne of Denmark, wife of James I. The original gate has recently been rebuilt stone by stone – and its statues (including Anne) replaced in their niches – in nearby Paternoster Square (see p. 38).

The sculptor of the Temple Bar Memorial griffin/dragon, Charles Bell Birch, survived the controversy and went on to make his own Queen Victoria (1893–6), which now presides over the entrance to Blackfriars Bridge. This larger-than-life statue stands in royal regalia, the star of India on the Queen's breast, her robes flowing over the pedestal edge (their texture

so well portrayed you can almost hear them rustle). The figure was presented 'to the citizens of London' by the Mayor of Derby, but its design goes back to a Golden Jubilee commission from the Maharana of Udaipur. At least eight casts were made, and they now stand in Derby, Newcastle-under-Lyme, Scarborough, Aberdeen, St Peter Port (Guernsey) and Adelaide (Australia) as well as London. The Udaipur original – in Carrara marble – was unveiled in India in 1889 but removed at independence in 1947.

As if these weren't enough, Victoria also looks out from the façade of Caxton Hall, opened as Westminster Town Hall in 1883 and renamed for the printer William Caxton in 1900. From 1903 it was a key base for the Suffragettes under Emmeline Pankhurst (p. 64) and a Suffragette memorial (a rather uninspiring bronze scroll) stands in a little public garden almost straight ahead of the statue.

During the Second World War Caxton Hall hosted Churchill's press conferences and was the site of a political assassination, while in the mid-twentieth century, as the local registry office, it saw many society marriages including those of Elizabeth Taylor, Roger Moore and Ringo Starr. It hosted the first meeting of the Homosexual Law Reform Society (1960) and of the National Front (1967). Frankly, the rather generic Queen Victoria just above the door is one of the least interesting things about the building.

Much more noticeable – and noticed – is the statue outside Croydon Library, part of the splendidly Victorian 1892 town hall that stands in sharp contrast to the concrete jungle around it. This Victoria's maker was another favourite of the Queen and sculpted her several times, along with other members of the royal family. The statue is akin to the figure at Buckingham Palace. Made at the same time, it was unveiled two years after the Queen's death by her sculptor daughter, Princess Louise (see above).

Here Victoria is clothed in a gloriously patterned dress with an effervescent lace collar, but the lady herself looks grim, not helped by the blackened bronze. Older locals seem to have a fondness for her, however, and a man in the pub courtyard next door told me, 'I've liked her since I was six. There used to be huge crowds here on poppy day, with people looking as much at Victoria as at the [neighbouring] war memorial.'

The Queen sits high atop an unusual war memorial in front of Westminster Abbey. This red granite column adorned with statuary was erected 'by their old schoolfellows' in memory of 19 named former pupils of Westminster School (which is in Dean's Yard, just through the Gilbert Scott gateway facing the column) who died in the Crimean War and Indian Mutiny. Their queen, Victoria, is less than gloriously celebrated here with an at-best mediocre statue, but even this is better than the one behind it, a dire, grim-faced effigy of the school's royal founder, Elizabeth I. Maybe it is not a tragedy that these column-top statues are difficult to see in detail.

Elevated and enthroned once more, Victoria sits atop the Foreign Office looking down on Whitehall.

The Queen holds an orb and a sceptre (which is slightly broken – not an ideal symbol for British diplomacy), and is flanked by a royal lion and unicorn and four standing classical figures. Only an overall impression of the Queen reaches us on the street below, but that is enough. She sits solid on the skyline, a personalised Britannia (p. 42) effectively communicating Victorian domination of her domain, local and global – which was, after all, the point of most of Victoria's many statues.

The Ugliest Statue in London? Bernard Shaw on Queen Victoria's statues

In 1919, the *Arts Gazette* asked its readers to identify the ugliest statue in London. The left-wing playwright  Bernard Shaw (1856–1950), by this time, in his own words, 'an old Victorian', did not come up with one effigy, but quickly identified a single subject, asking 'what crime Queen Victoria committed' to be so misrepresented 'as she is the length and breadth of her dominions'. She was, he pointed out, 'a tiny woman', but *our national passion for telling lies on every public subject has led to her being represented as an overgrown monster. The sculptors seem to have assumed that she inspired everything that was ugliest in the feminine fiction of her reign . . . Now if this were a bold republican realism which disdained courtly sycophancy, it would be at least courageous, if unkind. But it is pure plastic calumny. Queen Victoria was a little woman with great decision of manner and a beautiful speaking voice which she used in public extremely well. She carried herself very well. All young people now believe that she was a huge heap of a woman . . . How could they think anything else, with a statue at every corner shrieking these libels at them? . . . I blush for British sculpture, and long for a trip in a bombing aeroplane to remove Victoria's lying reproaches from the face of her land.* He perhaps had at the front of his mind the statue

of the queen on the Victoria Memorial outside Buckingham Palace – though as he notes there are many others. He might perhaps have made an exception for the Kensington Palace statue – though he didn't – and he might have liked the one in Victoria Square, but he'd have had to live to 150 to see it.

A political republican, Shaw was an unlikely defender of the monarch, but he clearly had a sneaking admiration for Victoria, particularly for how she survived her (specifically female) controlled and closeted Victorian upper-class upbringing. During her Golden Jubilee in 1887, Shaw wished the queen would list 'the lies a woman must either believe or pretend to believe before she can graduate in polite society as a well-brought-up lady'.

'Think of the young lady of 70 years ago,' he continued:

systematically and piously lied to by parents, governesses,

clergymen, servants, everybody; and slapped, sent to bed . . . at every rebellion of her common sense and natural instinct . . . against sham religion, sham propriety, sham decency, sham knowledge and sham ignorance.

Surely every shop window picture of 'the girl Queen' of 1837 must tempt the Queen of 1897 to jump out of her carriage and write up under it, 'Please remember that there is not a woman earning 24 shillings a week as a clerk today who is not ten times better educated than this unfortunate girl was when the crown dropped on her head, and left her to reign by her mother wit and the advice of a parcel of men who to this day have not sense enough to manage a Jubilee, let alone an Empire.'

St Ethelburga (or Æthelburh) Stone, 1892–5

By Nathaniel Hitch

All Hallows by the Tower, Byward Street, EC3R 5BJ

St Ethelburga (birthdate unknown, died after 686) was the first woman to lead a monastic order in England, and she stands above the door of the City of London's oldest church, which she established in 675. She was also a healer, diplomat and educator, especially of girls; not bad for a seventh-century woman who was originally sent to a religious community by her brother after she refused an arranged marriage.

Whether this was punishment, her choice or something in between isn't clear, but she certainly made the most of it, and her brother came to value her highly. He was Earconwald (or Erkonwald) – also later a saint – and in the 660s he founded two religious orders: one in Chertsey which he ran, and one in Barking, Essex, of which Ethelburga was abbess. This was a double abbey, so she was leading both men and women.

They cared for the sick during an outbreak of plague, and provided the only social care for the local populace. The Venerable Bede, writing about half a century after her death, said Ethelburga 'showed herself in all respects worthy . . . by her own holy life and by her regular and pious care of those under her rule'.

In 675 Earconwald became Bishop of London, and gave Ethelburga a plot of land on which to build a London chapel for Barking Abbey. The first church would have been of wood, but stone soon followed. Inside today's church stands a Saxon arch dated to the late seventh or early eighth century, incorporating Roman tiles and dressed stones salvaged from abandoned Londinium, the Roman city that covered

Twenty-first-century icon of St Ethelburga holding a model of the 'her' London church (inside the church).

this area until about 410.

Barking church, now All Hallows by the Tower (it's next to the Tower of London), has been here ever since. It survived the Great Fire – Samuel Pepys climbed its spire to watch 'the saddest sight of desolation that I ever saw' – but by the 1880s it was crumbling. Restoration brought a new north porch topped with three Victorian statues, including the Virgin Mary and St Ethelburga.

Ethelburga holds an abbess's crozier and a Bible. 'Her costume is wildly inappropriate', says All Hallows' history officer, Adey Grummet: 'wimples weren't worn until centuries later'. No matter; Grummet admires Ethelburga. 'She was a woman of steel, organised but compassionate. And in those early days of Anglo-Saxon Christianity (the diocese of London was only established in 604), with no set ways, she had to be a creative thinker too. What's not to admire?'

Sarah Siddons White marble, 1897

By Léon-Joseph Chavalliaudt
Paddington Green, W2 1NB

I first knew Sarah Siddons as a large girls' comprehensive school that, visiting aged 11, I found a bit intimidating. And I didn't even know it was said to be haunted by the eponymous 'Queen of Drury Lane' wearing a blue dress and a small hat.

One of the first modern-style celebrities, the actress Sarah Siddons (1755–1831) is buried in the neighbouring churchyard, and on the green opposite she sits, larger than life, in glowing white marble. This is the oldest statue of a named non-royal woman in London. And according to leading actor-manager

Henry Irving, who commissioned and unveiled it in 1897 (more than 65 years after her death), it was also the capital's first memorial to an actor.

Time has not been kind to Siddons. She now

sits hemmed in by modern construction (the church is the only building she would recognise), with the five-lane A40 roaring metres from her feet.

In 2011 vandals badly damaged the statue, including breaking off her nose (Gainsborough might have approved; it is said that while painting her portrait he exclaimed, 'Confound the nose, there's no end to it!'). Rescue and repair came only in 2019.

Siddons looks pretty fed up. But then a grin would hardly be appropriate for the woman known as 'the greatest tragedian', most famous for her unusually sympathetic portrayal of Lady Macbeth. Perhaps surprisingly, she also played Hamlet several times.

Her pose here is inspired by Sir Joshua Reynolds' 1784–5 portrait, *Sarah Siddons as the Tragic Muse*. She holds a dagger in her hand, and beneath her chair grimaces the mask of tragedy.

She knew tragedy of her own. Five of her seven children pre-deceased her, and her marriage disintegrated. On the other hand, born into the theatrical Kemble family, she rose from lady's maid and jobbing actress – initially quite unsuccessful – to mega-stardom. Lionised, well-paid and painted by most of the leading artists of the day, she had a carefully curated public image that went well beyond the theatre. Audience members were known to faint from 'Siddons fever'.

Having retired to Paddington, Siddons died of a skin infection (pre-antibiotics) and 5,000 people attended her funeral. I wonder if her ghost still haunts Westminster College, which has replaced the Sarah Siddons School.

Supreme Court Statuary Portland stone, 1913

Statuary by Henry Fehr (1867–1940), architect James Gibson (1861–1951)

Parliament Square, SW1P 3BD

No stand-alone statue of a woman graced Parliament Square until Millicent Fawcett in 2018 (p. 134), but stone statues of women have long looked down on proceedings here; they just aren't of real women. The 'Art Nouveau Gothic' façade of the Supreme Court, opened in 1913 as the Middlesex Guildhall, sports an array of niches filled with females, symbolising everything from the skill of architecture to the virtue of justice.

One real woman features, but not in 3D: a delicate

relief shows Lady Jane Grey (1536/7–54) being offered the crown of England. Hers is not a life to emulate. A learned young woman, she became a political pawn, was made queen for nine days, then imprisoned and executed.

All the other women are role models of sorts. A bold Britannia (see also p. 42) stands above the main entrance, flanked by female personifications of a range of skills – from law (with a scroll) to literature, seafaring (with a ship) and sculpture – mostly at the time considered beyond the wit of women. These females, then, are here to inspire men. Be grateful for small mercies: at least these ones aren't naked (see p. 100).

That said . . . the south façade balcony (opposite Westminster Abbey) is supported from below by a buxom host of near-horizontal angels. More like ship's figureheads, they look as if their breasts are about to bounce down to meet us. The furthest figure's bosom protrudes over a shield depicting the scales of justice, a subject you might expect to have been treated with less levity on a building that always housed a court of law.

Even when the building opened, the sculptor was regarded as having got away with a lot, but the architect was delighted. Amid 'austere and formal' Gothic surroundings, he said, he wanted 'a dainty piece of ornament . . . with a modern spirit of freshness'.

Much of the décor is playful, including some charming half-figures that emerge almost organically from the window lintels, the females including Art with a palette and perhaps Agriculture sporting a sheaf of corn. The back of the building is more serious. Atop the entrance originally used by defendants is blindfold Truth flanked by smaller figures of Honesty and Justice – all of them women.

The seriousness extends appropriately to the front door, 'guarded' – though there were then no women lawyers or judges – by female figures of Prudence and, with the downturned sword, Justice.

Susanna Wesley Red cedar wood, 2022

By Simon O'Rourke (b. 1978)

East Finchley Methodist Church, High Rd, N2 8AJ

See also: Catherine Booth, Salvationist 'Army Mother' (p. 52)

This totemic statue, marvellously different from most memorials, is carved from the remains of a red cedar tree in the church's little front garden. It honours 'the Mother of Methodism', Susanna Wesley (1669–1742) – mother both metaphorically and literally. Two of her sons, John and Charles, founded this Nonconformist Christian movement.

Despite Methodism spreading to 80 million people worldwide, this is apparently the first statue of Susanna Wesley anywhere. Commissioned for the church's bicentennial, it happened because, says Church Steward Jane Ray, 'The bare branches looked to us like Susanna's welcoming outstretched arms.'

Susanna was born the twenty-fifth of twenty-five children in London's Spitalfields. Her father was a Christian dissenter who encouraged independent thinking even in daughters, and at the age of 13 Susanna showed she'd learned well by leaving his Presbyterian church for the Church of England. At 19 she married Samuel Wesley, a C-of-E clergyman also of Dissenter stock.

It wasn't an easy life. Of their 19 children, nine died in infancy. Three sons and seven daughters survived. Susanna (somehow) gave each child time and educated them assiduously. She condemned the then prevalent habit of teaching girls sewing before reading, and one daughter became the poet Mehetabel Wesley Wright.

Samuel was not a reliable partner. He spent time in prison for debt and, after an argument with Susanna over the right of King William to rule, left the family for a year. In 1709 their Lincolnshire rectory home burned down (possibly through arson), young John only just escaping.

Absent again in 1712, Samuel appointed a caretaker

curate. The congregation, bored by his preaching, soon abandoned his services for Susanna's Sunday afternoon family prayers. When the curate complained of her 'kitchen conventicle' and Samuel asked her to desist, she refused, stopping only when Samuel returned. The episode, among others, left its mark on her soon-to-be-influential sons.

John Wesley first gave a woman a preaching licence in 1761, and in 1784 he removed 'obey' from the marriage vows to be used by American Methodists. In a sermon two years later, he railed against 'the maxim' that women should be seen but not heard, and be brought up 'as if only designed for agreeable playthings!' 'No,' he wrote, 'horrid cruelty . . . I know not how any women of sense and spirit can submit to it.'

His mother now stands, emerging organically from a tree trunk carved with leaves and woodland animals, pointing the way into the church he founded.

Sustrans Portrait Benches Corten steel cutouts, 2011–13

If you include 2D metal cut-outs (and why not), then the cycling and walking charity Sustrans has been responsible for a significant increase in London's (and the UK's) count of statues of women.

Each Portrait Bench – a seat plus standing figures – celebrates three 'local heroes' chosen by area residents. Six of the seven London installations include a woman (in one case, two women), and they are marvellously diverse and mostly surprisingly recognisable.

Born in Croydon, Peggy Ashcroft (1907–91) now stands slightly incongruously on a limelight-lacking back street, though it isn't far from the Ashcroft Theatre, named after her. Overcoming parental disapproval, Ashcroft went to drama school at 16 and quickly began a stellar career in British theatre lasting more than half a century. She was as comfortable in Brecht as Shakespeare and won multiple awards including, aged 77, a BAFTA and an Oscar for David Lean's film *A Passage to India* (1984).

Double Olympic-gold-medal-winning boxer Nicola Adams (b. 1982) started her sport aged 12 when her mother, desperate for after-school childcare, enrolled her and her brother in a boxing class. She faced plenty of 'women don't box' discrimination, but was soon representing the Haringey Police Community Boxing Club (near here).

When she started to compete overseas, money became a problem and she took all sorts of work – as an extra in soap operas, in construction – until finally receiving Olympic Committee funding from 2009. The investment paid off. In 2011 she became European champion, and at the 2012 London

Olympics Adams took the first ever Olympic gold in women's boxing (which had just become an Olympic sport). She continued to win every title available to a flyweight female until, with an eye injury that meant further boxing risked her sight, she retired in 2019. She now has a child with her girlfriend and has turned her attention to acting.

Phyllis Pearsall MBE (with Michael Caine and a bike representing cycling campaigner Barry Mason), Greenland Dock, at the end of Brunswick Quay opposite the Moby Dick pub, SE16 7PT

In 1935 a painter called Phyllis Pearsall went to a party. She was very late, she said, having got lost on the way. This led, so the story goes, to the A-Z, London's twentieth-century Google Maps (though without that handy blue dot). Her father was also involved, and his Geographer's

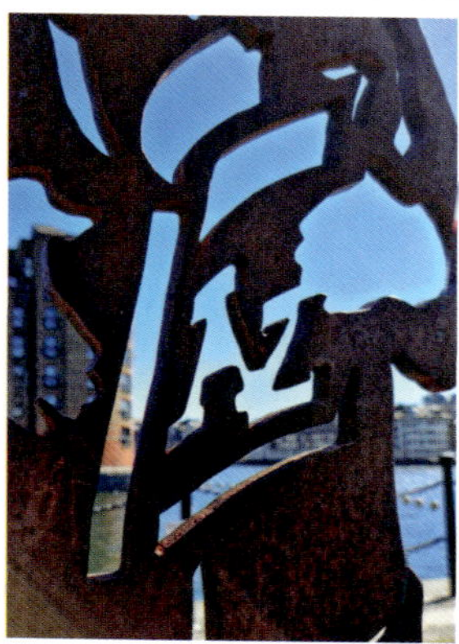

Map Company printed the resulting map book – though he put her in charge. A lifelong Londoner, Pearsall (1906–96) tramped thousands of miles through the capital's 23,000 streets, pencil in hand, and worked for the company until she was 93. Look closely and you can see the A-Z in her cutout's hands.

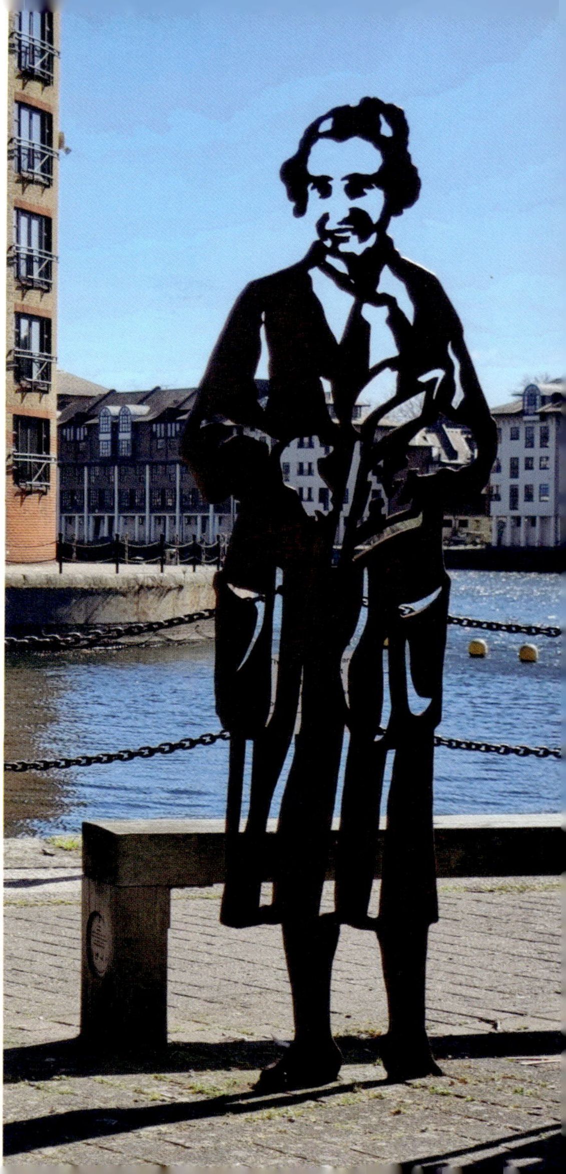

Seacole (1805–81) lived her later years in Paddington and finally died here. She isn't buried in the closest churchyard, but in St Mary's Catholic Cemetery up the Harrow Road in Kensal Rise. More about her on p. 126.

Daughter of Suffragette founder Emmeline Pankhurst (p. 64), Sylvia (1882–1960) was not always in agreement with her mother but was an equally active campaigner for women's rights. She is seen here handing out leaflets, with campaign text printed into her cutout. Trained as an artist, she saw 'so much distress' while painting working-class women that she

became a full-time activist. Feminist, socialist (but not a fan of Bolshevism), and anti-colonialist (especially in Ethiopia), she worked hard to help the women of the East End, 'that great abyss of poverty' (her words), to act collectively to improve their lives. Her name and picture can also be seen on the Millicent Fawcett statue in Parliament Square (p. 134).

Another Suffragette, Garrud (1872–1971) contributed quite differently to the cause. Though she looks conventional here in her long skirt with a book and a Suffragette sash, she was one of the first female martial arts teachers in the Western world. The UK's first woman to teach ju-jitsu, she ran a martial arts centre and trained Suffragettes in self-defence. She was instrumental in creating their unit of pre-World War I female bodyguards, whose methods were nicknamed by the press, 'Suffrajitsu'.

Keen (1868–1942) was 'the Angel of Islington'. She is shown here holding a baby because she saved so many local infants' lives. In 1913, 10 per cent of babies born in the borough died before their fifth birthday, so Keen set up the North Islington Infant Welfare Centre and School for Mothers. She lost two sons of her own in the World War I, but continued her work, saving the lives of many other mothers' children. The centre continues today as the Manor Gardens Welfare Trust.

Edith Garrud demonstrates the art of ju-jitsu

Three Graces

Terracotta, 1875–80. By Joseph Kremer
(c.1833–82)
Four statues of the Three Graces flanking two
gateways onto the driveway of 1–10 Cambridge
Gate, Regent's Park, NW1 4JX

Gilded aluminium, 1992. By Rudy Weller
(b. 1956).
The Three Graces or Daughters of Helios,
Criterion Building, Piccadilly Circus, corner of
Haymarket

The Three Graces are usually described as daughters of Zeus, but sometimes as offspring of the sun god Helios and Aegle (daughter of Zeus). Also called the Charities, they are goddesses of charm and beauty, associated with joy and gratitude – definitely characters you want to have around. The trio is most often named as Aglaea (meaning 'shining one'), Euphrosyne ('merriment') and Thalia ('abundance', linked to festivities), and presented as an interlaced group of graceful (of course) women dancing in the nude.

The Cambridge Gate Graces are classically posed but fully draped (the wealthy Victorian residents of Regent's Park might not all have appreciated 12 naked ladies on their doorstep). Each group is a little different. Indeed, it has been credibly suggested that the four compositions represent the seasons. One group is extra-draped and adorned with holly and ivy (winter), one with vines and grapes (autumn), the third features a sickle and cut corn (summer), and the final group small flowers and vegetation (spring). Perhaps the Graces here are merged with their half-sisters the Horae, three goddesses of the seasons who, in Homer's *Iliad*, are the gatekeepers of Olympus.

The Piccadilly Circus Graces or Daughters of Helios

are, by contrast, traditional only in their nudity. These elegant figures dive from the sixth-storey roof, high above a ground-level sculpture of the Horses of Helios, said to daily draw the sun god's chariot east to west across the sky. These glittering golden Graces certainly look sunlit.

'Piccadilly and Leicester Square were my playground as a boy growing up in London,' the sculptor Rudy Weller told me,

so I put my life and feelings into this work. The Daughters of Helios are soaring . . . free from earthly constrictions. They are the spirit of life – beautiful, joyful, creative, peaceful, and their golden bodies reflect the life-giving rays from the sun. We need beauty and poetry in our lives, and Piccadilly is the heart of London where dreams are made (and broken) . . . full of excitement and adventure.

Trinity Buoy Wharf

Works by Andrew Baldwin (B. 1961) including:
Vitruvian Woman (kinetic sculpture, bronze and recycled elements, 2005); caryatids (steel, 2015)

64 Orchard Place, E14 0JW

Amid the historic Thameside workshops (1803–1988) of lighthouse organisation Trinity House – and beside London's only surviving lighthouse – stand a series of kinetic and post-industrial sculptures, many of them women. All are by Andrew Baldwin, artist-

in-residence at what is now a contemporary arts centre. A shifting body of work (for sale) is complemented by a couple of permanent pieces featuring female figures.

Vitruvian Woman, which the artist calls Wendy after the woman who modelled for it, is a bronze nude divided into seven parts, six of which circulate mesmerically, coming together only once every three-and-a-half hours into a whole woman. It clearly references traditional idealised female nudes, while the title comes from Leonardo da Vinci's *Vitruvian Man*, which depicts several positions at once and marries art and science. A former blacksmith, Baldwin

uses recycled industrial elements to hark back – appropriately for the location – to Victorian engineering and industrialisation.

Vitruvian Woman, he says, 'is about a friend of mine [not the model Wendy]'. A fragmented personality? 'Aren't we all . . . but it wasn't a good relationship.' He generally works from live models, and most of his works are women because (like Henry Moore, p. 114, whose work he doesn't like) he says they have more shape than men. He doesn't get complaints about his female nudes, he adds, 'but I've got a lot of stick for the [occasional] naked man – usually, strangely, from women . . . And one lady complained about one of the women not having pubic hair – well, the model was a modern woman and she didn't!'

Above the sculpture-filled courtyard two shining silver caryatids prop up a modern external stairway. They were modelled on a young woman who worked in the café opposite and they are constructed from off-cut steel strips creating a sparkling contemporary art-industrial take on the traditional female architectural support – the classical caryatid.

The Tuckshop Tanner Bronze, 2017

By Jessica Wetherly (b. 1989)

Archbishop's Park, SE1 7LG

Appropriately facing a children's playground, this statue is both a generic tribute to human kindness and a specific memorial to Lizzie Lambert, who ran the school tuckshop that occupied this site until 1974. On the children's birthdays, Lambert would (at least until decimalisation in 1971) give them a sixpence – a tanner – and on the statue's pregnant belly is the pattern of an oversized sixpence.

Lambert's son Charlie, a banker turned London cabbie (like his father before him), still lives in the area and walks his dogs in the park. 'I always rub the sixpence for luck and say hello to the statue. I do feel mum is there. And my brother and sister's ashes are scattered around the statue, so it's important to me.' If he looks over the figure's left shoulder, he says, he can see the house where he was born. The family has lived in the area for generations, and Charlie is delighted that his mother's statue commemorates 'a school dinner lady who then ran a tuckshop – an ordinary bod'.

The statue was commissioned by the Archbishop's Park Community Trust, a local charity supporting the park, which was donated to the people of the area in 1901 by the Archbishop of Canterbury. Jessica Wetherly, the sculptor, says she felt particularly honoured to win this commission because she herself

Jessica Wetherly creates the cast for the statue of Lizzie Lambert.

'comes from a family of hard-working working-class women and teachers'.

She deliberately left the surface of the bronze unsmoothed because 'we have a strong tradition of Victorian sculpture in the UK, and it can feel a bit stiff'. She wanted her statue to be 'more open', to retain some of the energy of the clay modelling and be 'softened into the landscape'.

Slightly camouflaged amid the surface texture, the rough circle of the sixpence is recognisable by its design of a rose, thistle, leek and shamrock, representing the four home nations of the UK. This was what sixpences looked like for their last couple of decades, when Lizzie Lambert was handing them out to the schoolkids. The tanner was the smallest silver coin, typical children's pocket money, and had quite a place in British culture. From Tommy Steele singing *Half a Sixpence* in 1963 to Queen guitarist Brian May using tanners in place of plectrums, affection for the sixpence seemed universal. And it was often, as here, associated with good luck and prosperity.

Twiggy Bronze, 2012

By Neal French (b.1933)
Bourdon Place, W1K 3AB

Tucked away in a cobbled Mayfair mews, Twiggy poses for the fashion photographer Terence Donovan, while a woman loaded with boutiquey shopping bags pauses – like us – to watch. These life-size bronzes, though texturally minimalist, are nonetheless evocative of

a scene from London's Swinging Sixties. They're based on a photograph Donovan took in 1966 of the teenage Twiggy dressed in an oh-so-of-its-time Mary Quant outfit (note the tie), that went as viral as was possible in print.

Born Lesley Hornby in 1949 in Neasden (north-west London) to a carpenter and a factory worker, the petite, twig-thin 16-year-old was working as an assistant in a hair salon when she volunteered to model a new cut at Leonard of Mayfair. The resulting stylish short hair completed her soon-to-be-famous Peter Pan look, and the headshots on the salon wall quickly drew attention from the fashion journalist Deirdre McSharry. In the *Daily Express* she labelled Twiggy 'the face of '66 . . . the Cockney kid with a face to launch a thousand shapes'.

Twiggy's hairdresser boyfriend, ten years her senior, became her manager, and within a month she was in *Vogue*, within a year an international supermodel with three layers of false eyelashes, her own line of dresses and even (in America) Twiggy lunchboxes. The possible impact on girls' health of idolising a 41kg frame concerned some critics from the start, but for Twiggy this was simply her natural shape, and she thought everyone 'stark raving mad' for finding it sexy.

Still only just legally adult, she retired from modelling in 1970 declaring that 'You can't be a clothes hanger for your entire life.' She turned to film, starring first in her friend Ken Russell's

all-singing, all-dancing (she learned
fast!) *The Boyfriend* (1971), for which she
won two Golden Globes.

Twiggy went on to make a successful
long-term career across multiple
entertainment genres, releasing albums,
playing a wide variety of stage and screen
roles, hosting her own TV chat show and
more. She found time too to marry the
American actor Michael Witney and have
their daughter Carley in 1978. Witney,
an alcoholic, died of a heart attack just
six years later, and since 1988 Twiggy
has been married to the English actor
Leigh Lawson, whose name both she and
Carly took. So when Twiggy was given
a damehood in 2019, she became Dame
Lesley Lawson.

In 2012 it was Twiggy herself who
unveiled these statues in Mayfair where
it all began.

War...

Symbolic female figures are often enlisted in support of military prowess on monuments and memorials otherwise exclusively male. Frankly, women were fortunate not to fight and die as men did in the commemorated conflicts, though their role was often greater than acknowledged (see Women of World War II Memorial, p. 214, Florence Nightingale, p. 66, Edith Cavell, p. 58, Mary Seacole, p. 126, Noor Inayat Khan, p. 142, Violette Szabo, p. 200).

The symbolic women of war represent the celebrated virtues and achievements of the men, particularly as personifications of Victory, Honour and Peace – sometimes rolled into one. Symbols of valour may be masculine (see Marble Arch, p. 210, for instance), but women can also represent the fighting spirit, sporting military accoutrements like helmets, breastplates, shields or spears/tridents (see also Britannia, p. 42).

Female personifications of Victory date back to the Greek goddess Nike (literally meaning Victory), who became Victoria under the Romans and was worshipped by the Roman army. Nike was originally invoked by competing athletes and, legend tells us, became associated with military success after driving Zeus's chariot to victory in the Olympians' battle against the Titans. Promoted to Mount Olympus, she is linked to both Zeus and Athena.

Victory is usually depicted, now as then, in flowing drapes (sometimes rather thin). She often has wings (but not always), and holds a laurel wreath, traditionally awarded to victorious Ancient Greek athletes and Roman military leaders. Via the Renaissance, the rise of archaeology in the eighteenth century and the resulting Neoclassicism, Victorys (and other classical personifications) range across London (see also National Gallery & Marble Arch, p. 210).

Waterloo Place (SW1Y 4AN) provides an interesting cluster of different symbolic war women . . .

Waterloo Place

Lord Clyde memorial

A feminine Victory honours Field Marshall Colin Campbell, Lord Clyde, 'hero' of multiple colonial conflicts, on his 1867 memorial (by Carlo Marochetti). She poses in shapely breastplate and drapery, on a lion, as if modelling for some Victorian car ad. Or as a contemporary reviewer put it, 'in the manner of the cirque'.

Athenaeum Athena

Looking on is her mentor Athena, who stands in golden glory (by Edward Hodges Baily, 1829) above the Neoclassical portico of the Athenaeum, a 200-year-old members' club. Founded by and for leading men of science and the arts, the club invokes Athena as

the Greek goddess of wisdom, but she was a war goddess too, and sports a military helmet and spear. Despite its choice of female totem, the club did not admit women members until the twenty-first century.

Crimean War memorial

Honour makes an appearance in the middle of the road atop the huge 1861 Crimean War Memorial to 2,162 dead guardsmen – unusually, of all ranks. The sculptor, John Bell, insisted on Honour rather than Victory because, as he sensibly put it, 'We can retain honour, though we cannot always ensure victory.' It is not, however, easy to differentiate his Honour from Victory, and the figure came in for ridicule, as the multiple laurel wreaths she holds were said to make her look as if she was playing quoits.

Boer War Memorial

On the Mall at the bottom of Waterloo Place, atop the Royal Artillery Boer War Memorial (1910, SW1A 2BJ),

incidentally placed here rather than on Waterloo Place itself because the Athenaeum Club deemed it 'undesirable', we find a mash-up of Peace and Victory. The memorial is dominated by a bronze statue (by William Robert Colton) of the Angel of Peace calming a horse representing the spirit of war. Peace is bare-breasted (see Laid Bare, p. 100), which caused no controversy, and winged, which did. Initially the warhorse had wings and Peace did not, which the sculptor was asked to reverse. This done, he tweaked the design so one wing curved over the horse's back indicating Peace's dominance. The commissioning committee decided the wing looked broken and insisted it be re-erected. So Peace is almost indistinguishable from Winged Victory – though she does hold an olive branch in addition to her laurel wreath.

Islingtonian War Memorial
Bronze, by Bertram Mackennal, 1905.
SE corner of Highbury Fields (opposite the station), Highbury Crescent, N5 1RD

A young woman as Glory is the primary feature of this unusual war memorial – paid for by local people to commemorate some 100 of their number who died in the Boer War 1899–1903. Flanked by two cannons, she marches forward, triumphant, over a pile of military regalia, holding high a laurel wreath of victory.

Following the 2020 toppling of the Bristol statue of slave-owner Edward Colston and amid Black Lives Matter protests, the historian Neal Ascherson made a plea to protect this statue. Acknowledging that it glorified a colonial war in South Africa between 'two white nations exploiting black labour', he wrote that it 'remembers the poor lads who died in this completely stupid war'. Rather than remove

it, he said, another memorial should be added – he suggested a black woman – to commemorate those caught in the crossfire. No sign of this yet.

Victory, Queen Victoria Memorial
Outside Buckingham Palace

Unusually Victory is here enlisted in memory not of masculine military achievement but of her monarchical namesake, Queen Victoria (see also p. 164).

See also: National Gallery & Marble Arch (p. 210)

...and Peace

The olive branch as a symbol of peace dates back more than two-and-a-half millennia. It was then held by the Greek goddess Eirene (meaning 'peace' in Greek), later Roman Pax ('peace' in Latin), and represented

the plenty that peace could bring. Often this classical goddess also held a cornucopia (horn of plenty), sceptre and torch.

While the olive branch has become a universal peace symbol, and Peace almost always holds one, her personifications in London vary considerably. Two figures at either end of Piccadilly illustrate the range. Both are 'classical', but present us with entirely different ideas of Peace.

At Hyde Park Corner, Peace dominates the dramatic Quadriga (by Adrian Jones, designed 1891, placed here 1912) that tops Wellington Arch (W1J 7JZ). The arch was originally constructed in 1826–9 as a grand outer gateway to Buckingham Palace as well as a victory arch for Wellington's defeat of Napoleon. The largest bronze statue in Western Europe, the Quadriga's symbolism is akin to that on the Boer War Memorial (above). The huge Angel of Peace alights on a war chariot drawn by four powerful horses (the quadriga) and is, the sculptor explained, about to get the boy charioteer to 'rein in the horses'.

The model for Peace was Beatrice Stewart, a professional artists' model also employed by John Singer Sargent, Walter Sickert and Augustus John. By 1933 she had lost a leg in a car accident and was living nearby in Shepherd Market, Mayfair. Here she was the 'kind-hearted landlady' of a rather rowdy teenage Patrick Leigh Fermor, about to set out on the walk across Europe that he later turned into his book *A Time of Gifts*. In it he wrote, 'I can never pass the top of Constitution Hill without thinking of her and gazing up at the winged and wreath-bearing goddess sailing across the sky. As the pigeon flies it was under a minute from her windowsill.'

The original Quadriga design, called Triumph, displayed at the Royal Academy in 1891, had the angel holding a palm branch (classically associated

with victory). This was switched for an olive branch when the sculpture became associated with Edward VII, the 'Peacemaker King' (see p.35), who was closely involved in its choice for the arch. When he died ahead of its installation, the Quadriga became (as a plaque tells us), a memorial to him. Nonetheless, the statue remains a thoroughly triumphal Edwardian idea of Peace.

By contrast, in the garden of the church of St James's Piccadilly, a lone, human-sized figure of Peace stands at our level. Notably made after the horrors of the World War I (by Alfred Hardiman, c. 1926), she is barefoot and clothed in a simple dress. This figure harks back to Greek sculpture, its eyes even hollow like a statue that has survived from antiquity, but it is not conflated with Victory. This Peace holds an olive twig and her hands are up, vulnerable, palms open. She's still, calm and entirely un-triumphalist.

Peace on Equestrian Statue of Prince Albert
Bronze, by Charles Bacon, 1873,
Holborn Circus, EC1N 8AA

Beneath Prince Albert sits Peace in an unusually relaxed pose. She looks like a society lady – a rather daring one with her clothing falling suggestively open at the chest. On her head is

left: Peace by Alfred Hardiman, c.1926, erected here 1950 in memory of the sculptor, Southwood Memorial Garden, St James's Piccadilly, 197 Piccadilly, W1 J9L

a laurel wreath, while her hands hold a palm branch and a cornucopia. Beside her is a relief of Britannia handing out laurel wreaths at the prince's 1851 international Great Exhibition – celebrated here as an example of peaceful co-operation between nations.

She doesn't only sit beneath Prince Albert, though. Her head is in fact directly below the raised tail of his horse, which looks exactly as if it is about to poop on her. Was the sculptor (or installer) having a laugh at Albert's or the City's expense – or even making a point about Imperial 'peace' when Britain had been at war with someone somewhere for most of the century?

Peace on Hammersmith War Memorial
Bronze, by Henry Fehr, 1922. Eastern end of Shepherd's Bush Green, W12 8LB

A classic Peace-cum-Victory, this substantial winged figure alighting on a small globe carries a laurel wreath of victory in one hand and a raised sword (albeit pointed downwards) in the other.

See also: Queen Victoria as Peace (p. 167), Peace on the Victoria Memorial (p. 210), Peace with the Spoils of War on Marble Arch (p. 212), Peace memorial drinking fountain (p. 35).

Violette Szabo — SOE Memorial Bronze, 2009

By Karen Newman (b. 1951)

Queen's Walk, Albert Embankment, Lambeth, SE1 7JT

Also: Violette Szabo is remembered in a mural in Stockwell Memorial Garden, next to Bronze Woman (p. 48) and near her London home at 18 Burnley Rd.

In 2009 a memorial was unveiled to all members of SOE, the Special Operations Executive. Unusually – or perhaps in a sign of the times – the individual chosen to represent the group was a woman, Violette Szabo (1921–45).

'Churchill's secret army' was quietly recruited from 1940 for the dangerous work of sabotage and support of local resistance behind enemy lines. As the statue's plaque states, 470 agents were sent to France; 117 never came back. Thirty-nine of the agents were women, their gender – and the gender stereotyping of the time – making them less likely to be suspected.

Szabo's bust here looks a little like that of Noor Inayat Khan (p. 142), another young female SOE agent, perhaps because they are by the same sculptor. But Szabo's darker bronze figure stares more robustly out across the River Thames.

Born Violette Bushell in Paris to a French seamstress and British cabbie, Szabo had four brothers with whom her father taught her to shoot. Leaving school in Brixton aged 14, she worked in department stores until the outbreak of war, when she joined up, soon becoming Gunner Szabo.

At London's Bastille Day Parade of 1940, the 19-year-old Violette met the Free French soldier Etienne Szabo. They were married 42 days later, before he was deployed to North Africa. Their daughter was born in 1942, but never met her father, who was killed at El Alamein, prompting his widow to join the SOE. Her training reports were mixed, but this diminutive young woman (just 5'3") with a Cockney accent and mischievous demeanour apparently kept her comrades cheerful.

Violette Szabo's four-year-old daughter Tania wearing her mother's posthumous George Cross after receiving it from the King.

After her first mission
had to be aborted, Szabo was
parachuted back into France just
after D-Day to sabotage German
communication lines. The local
resistance was disorganised, and
she was soon arrested. Exactly
what happened is disputed. The
story goes that there was a gun
battle and Szabo, immobilised
by a twisted ankle, gave lethal
covering fire so her French
(male) colleague could escape –
until her ammunition ran out.
But this may be heroic fiction.

Either way, she was
interrogated, tortured and sent
to Ravensbrück concentration
camp where, after a period
of hard labour, cold and
starvation, she was executed
with a shot to the back of the
head. She was 23.

Szabo was awarded the
George Cross in 1946, which
was collected from George VI
by her four-year-old daughter,
Tania. Her fictionalised story is
told in the 1958 film *Carve Her
Name with Pride*.

Virginia Woolf

A peaky Virginia Woolf (1882–1941), reminiscent of her own Mrs Dalloway, looks pensively out across Tavistock Square gardens, while behind her (just as it does in her novel) London bustles past.

Woolf was living at 52 Tavistock Square (now the Tavistock Hotel) between 1924 and 1939 when she published much of her most famous work, including the novels *Mrs Dalloway* (1925) and *To the Lighthouse*

(1927) which she 'made up, as I sometimes make up my books . . . in a great, apparently involuntary, rush' while walking in this square.

The books were printed by the Hogarth Press, run by Virginia and her husband Leonard Woolf from their basement. They had started the press (which also first published T. S.

Eliot's *The Waste Land* in 1922) while living at Hogarth House, Richmond (1914–24), and recently the riverside here has gained an entirely different evocation of Virginia, looking calm and relaxed.

The statue's location was briefly criticised as 'insensitive' because in 1941 Woolf drowned herself in a river. But that wasn't this river. It was the Ouse in East Sussex, where the Woolfs moved to escape the Blitz, and she is known to have enjoyed walking her dog along the Thames here.

Indeed, she found rivers aided contemplation. In *A Room of One's Own* (1929), based on talks she gave at Cambridge University's two women's colleges, she wrote, "When you asked me to speak about Women

and Fiction, I sat down on the banks
of a river and began to wonder what
the words meant.'

Woolf should not be defined by
her death, though her mental health
was fragile from childhood. She was
sexually abused by a half-brother and
lost her mother aged 13 triggering her
first mental collapse. Further family
deaths and breakdowns followed
but Woolf, along with her three full
siblings, nonetheless became the
core of the Bloomsbury Group of
accomplished, irreverent, mould-
breaking, though often tormented
artists and intellectuals.

Unlike her brothers, Virginia
and her sister (artist Vanessa Bell)
were not sent to public school
and Cambridge, just one of the
disadvantages of being female
Virginia deeply resented. *In A Room
of One's Own*, however, she considers
London's statues glorifying men and
war and her anger at the patriarchy
begins to turn to pity and liberation
(see p. 204).

So it is particularly gratifying that
she now has two London statues all
of her own.

Virginia Woolf contemplates London's statues

In *A Room of One's Own* (1929), Virginia Woolf (p. 202) looks at some of London's macho statues and war memorials and reflects on male privilege. Having been left £500 a year by a distant aunt, giving her a previously undreamed-of independence from men, she finds herself a little more forgiving of the patriarchy and the men perpetuating it:

Their education had been in some ways as faulty as my own. It had bred in them defects as great. True, they had money and power, but only at the cost of harbouring in their breasts an eagle, a vulture, forever tearing the liver out and plucking at the lungs – the instinct for possession, the rage for acquisition which drives them to desire other people's fields and goods perpetually; to make frontiers and flags; battleships and

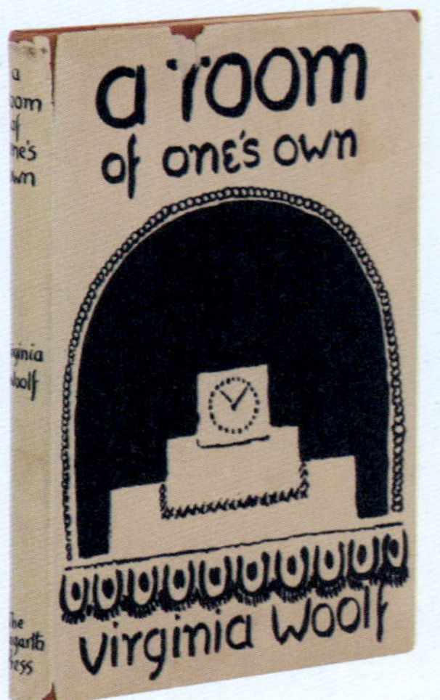

poison gas; to offer up their own lives and their children's lives. Walk through the Admiralty Arch (I had reached that monument), or any other avenue given up to trophies and cannon, and reflect upon the kind of glory celebrated there. Or watch in the spring sunshine the stockbroker and the great barrister going indoors to make money and more money and more money when

it is a fact that five hundred pounds a year will keep one alive in the sunshine. These are unpleasant instincts to harbour, I reflected. They are bred of the conditions of life; of the lack of civilisation, I thought, looking at the statue of the Duke of Cambridge, and in particular at the feathers in his cocked hat, with a fixity that they have scarcely ever received before. And, as I realised these drawbacks, by degrees fear and bitterness modified themselves into pity and toleration; and then in a year or two, pity and toleration went, and the greatest release of all came, which is freedom to think of things in themselves. That building, for example, do I like it or not? Is that picture beautiful or not? Is that in my opinion a good book or a bad? Indeed my aunt's legacy unveiled the sky to me, and substituted for the large and imposing figure of a gentleman, which Milton recommended for my perpetual adoration, a view of the open sky.

A Room of One's Own, Chapter 2 (1929)

Warm Shores Bronze, 2022

They stand larger than life outside Hackney Town Hall, a young black man and a slightly older black woman – definitely female despite the only indicator being her more feminine blouse. Unveiled on National Windrush Day, 22 June 2022 – the same day as the National Windrush Monument (see p. 208) – these giant figures are composites of 30 Hackney residents, aged 20 to 91, with links to the Windrush generation.

The South London sculptor Thomas J. Price, whose 'Windrush' grandmother came to the UK from Jamaica as a nurse, interviewed each person and took digital 3D images before combining them into this Caribbean-heritage 'everyman' and 'everywoman'. His aim: to honour the 'pioneering individuals' who had the courage to travel across the world, 'on the promise of a warm welcome'.

'This is where the title *Warm Shores* comes from,' Price has said: 'leaving a warm, safer home, a warm climate, and the waters of the Caribbean and expecting a warm welcome – perhaps not finding that warm welcome.'

Twenty-one per cent of Hackney residents are black (and nearly half non-white), with almost one in ten considering themselves Caribbean. This sculpture is the second part of the borough's Windrush memorial commission, that also included Veronica Ryan's Turner Prize-winning *Custard*

The unveiling of *Warm Shores* in 2022.

Apple . . . (see above), a group of oversized bronze and marble Caribbean fruit and veg that was, at its unveiling in 2021, London's first permanent public statue to the Windrush generation.

As for *Warm Shores*, 'It's not a monument,' says Price, 'it's a celebration.' The figures stand on the ground, not on a pedestal, and are casually dressed, but their monumental scale (2.75m), high-status material (bronze) and prominent political position at the town hall clearly reference more traditional statues, particularly of (male) colonial leaders.

National Windrush Monument

Bronze, unveiled on the fifth Windrush Day, 22 June 2022

By Basil Watson (b. 1958)

Waterloo Station, SE1 8SQ

See also with Windrush connections: Joy Battick interview (p. 88), Bronze Woman (p. 48), Warm Shores (p. 206) And: Basil Watson's brother Raymond made the Soweto memorial statue, *First Child*, in Brixton.

The woman is at the heart of this family group celebrating the Windrush Generation – half a million migrants who arrived in the UK from Caribbean colonies between the 1948 docking of the *Empire Windrush* and 1971. The female figure holds the hand of the male (who steps optimistically forward) and the head of the child (who looks uncertainly back). The woman/wife/mother appears neither over-confident nor fearful, moves neither forward nor back – though, her swinging skirt makes clear, neither is she still.

Clearly individual, she is also the little group's glue, support and centre.

The family will need this security as they discover a 'Mother Country' less motherly than expected. Racism was rife, and the Windrush generation faced an uphill struggle. Many nonetheless made successful lives in Britain, and it is this 'heroism' the sculptor, Basil Watson, aimed to capture.

The figures stand on seven period suitcases, their bundled-up lives carried across the ocean. They are dressed in 'Sunday best'. A *Daily Mirror* reporter, surprised by the 'expensive suits' worn by Afro-Caribbeans disembarking the *Windrush* was told, 'The very poor can't leave Jamaica. They must have twenty-eight pounds [about £1,200 today] for their passage, and another five pounds on them when they sail. It wasn't poverty that brought me here.'

Many women arrived alone, 'sent for' by male relatives or taking up jobs as nurses or 'HD' – 'household domestic' (something of a catch-all).

There were also lawyers, musicians, and artists like Watson's father Barrington, who came to attend London's Royal College of Art – meeting Basil's mother on the ship.

The monument is personal too for Floella, Baroness Benjamin, Chair of the Windrush Commemoration Committee that, with community consultation, selected the design. Born in Trinidad in 1949, she says, 'I remember well my own moment of arrival, as a ten-year-old,' she says – 'stepping off the train and standing on platform nineteen at Waterloo Station.'

The 1971 Immigration Act tightened controls on immigration but gave already-resident Commonwealth citizens indefinite leave to remain. Government record-keeping failures, however, meant that many Windrush-era migrants were later wrongly labelled illegal. This 'Windrush Scandal' led to appalling injustices, including deportation, divided families and denial of healthcare. Despite official apologies, it has taken far too long to resolve.

No monument can compensate for that, but this statue is seen as a kind of recognition, and it is daily appreciated by many in transit through Waterloo Station, whether or not they have direct connections to the Windrush Generation.

Women of the National Gallery — and Marble Arch

See also: Fourth Plinth (p. 22), War and Peace (p. 194)

The National Gallery building (1830s) is such a landmark in Trafalgar Square that few notice its architectural statuary – all of which is female. This inattention may be just as well, since closer inspection reveals something odd about the art on the outside of our premier artistic institution.

There are several personifications of Victory (see also p. 194), an armed Minerva and, above the main entrance, rather generic bare-breasted figures representing Europe and Asia seated on a horse and a camel. What do all these – and their military symbolism – have to do with a national art gallery?

Well, not much. And even the two winged figures personifying Painting (above the Getty entrance) are simply Victorys who have swapped spear and shield for paintbrush and palette. The fact is that all this statuary was originally made not for the gallery but for Marble Arch, a triumphal monument to the British victory over Napoleon.

The continental women ceremoniously display a wreath-framed oval – but it's empty. It was intended to carry a portrait of war hero the Duke of Wellington, but was repurposed before the portrait was installed. Not so the head of Admiral Lord Nelson that once adorned the shield of Britannia, made by John Flaxman for Marble Arch, which was converted into the National Gallery's Minerva (now seated above a doorway facing St Martins-in-the-Fields). The conversion was done by the sculptor Edward Hodges Baily, who had to literally chip the head of Nelson away. He made amends to the naval hero later, sculpting the 5.5m statue for his eponymous column.

Baily probably also made all the Victorys (the Paintings, plus Victorys either side of *Europe and Asia*,

Europe and Asia, designed by John Nash, sculpted by Charles Rossi, National Gallery portico.

Minerva, National Gallery. Originally *Britannia* by John Flaxman (1755—1826), converted by Edward Hodges Baily.

and one above each of the Getty and West entrances).
The West door Victory is flanked by two unidentified
classically draped women – and all three are ill-
proportioned for their niches. Victory only just fits,
while the flanking figures look meagre in their spaces
– another nod to the statues' origins elsewhere.

Marble Arch was designed by John Nash in 1827 in
response to Napoleon's triumphal arches in Paris and
as a ceremonial entrance to Buckingham House, which
Nash was converting into a palace for George IV.

The three Home Nations on Marble Arch, newly unveiled in
May 2025 after restoration.

Many of the statues (all classically themed) were
complete but not installed by 1830 when the king
died. The Prime Minister, Wellington (yes, the
same), promptly sacked Nash for overspending and
appointed Edward Blore to do a more economical
job. Blore used only some of Nash's statues and, in
the spirit of economy (government cuts are nothing
new), the architect William Wilkins was told in 1835 to

make do with Blore's cast-offs for his National Gallery.

By 1850, after Blore added the current façade to Buckingham Palace for Queen Victoria, Marble Arch was moved stone by stone to become a grand entrance to Hyde Park for the 1851 Great Exhibition. Here it remains, now isolated by traffic but still reachable.

One might think Blore took full advantage of his first dibs on the statues. On the North side of the arch a female trio (by Richard Westmacott) represents England in Britannia's helmet, Ireland holding a harp, and Scotland with a shield of St Andrew (and a barely draped bum that seems carved with more artistry than her face). Amid swirling drapery stands a curvaceous, near-naked Peace with Trophies of War (see also Peace, p. 197).

On the South side, by Baily, the women are more decorous, though less aesthetically interesting, and triumphal symbols are in their element: six reliefs of Victory (yes, more) surround the Angel of Peace, which faces Plenty across a flame of liberty; a female Virtue accompanies Valour (a Roman soldier).

It is perhaps no bad thing that most of the National Gallery's visitors concentrate on the extraordinary art inside.

National Gallery, architect: William Wilkins, opened 1938.

The Women of World War II Bronze, 2005

This striking black bronze monument stands in the middle of the road just north of the national war memorial, the Cenotaph, which it rather overshadows. Replacing a statue of the sixteenth-century privateer Walter Raleigh (moved to Greenwich), this monument proclaims in gold letters – reminiscent of the font used on ration books – that it has been 'raised to commemorate the vital work done by over seven million women during World War II'.

By 1943 nine out of ten single women aged 20 to 30 had been conscripted and others volunteered. Most became 'land girls' working on farms, factory workers making munitions, drivers, mechanics or air raid wardens, but 640,000 were members of the armed forces, 55,000 of them bearing guns.

Recognition was a long time coming. This memorial was unveiled by Queen Elizabeth II (p. 160), herself a wartime driver and mechanic in the Auxiliary Territorial Service (ATS), to coincide with the sixtieth anniversary of the end of the war. It was also just two days after the 7/7 London terrorist bombings.

The statue was dedicated by Baroness (Betty) Boothroyd, former speaker of the House of Commons and patron of the trust that made the monument happen. She raised some of the money by doing a celebrity episode of the TV quiz show *Who Wants to be a Millionaire?* The famous wartime singer Dame Vera Lynn was vice-patron and also attended the unveiling, watching a flypast of planes and helicopters all piloted and crewed by women.

This monument is as much about absence as presence. Seventeen sets of clothing, representing women's roles in the war, hang as if from pegs. Many are identifiable uniforms, including those of the ATS,

Members of the WAAF packing parachutes during World War II.

Women's Royal Naval Service (WRENS), Women's Auxiliary Air Force (WAAF), Women's Land Army, Red Cross nurses, Air Wardens, police and fire service. There's even a welder's mask.

Visually inspired by a photograph of a cloakroom at a 1940s dance hall, the sculptor John Mills – himself evacuated from London as a child after his mother joined the fire service – was 'interested in the concept of these women hanging up their uniforms and going back to their normal lives after the end of the war' when men returned and reclaimed 'their' roles. Some, though, also see in the empty uniforms the absence of those who died.

Statue Safari 1: Westminster

Outside the front of Victoria Station you'll see the Victoria Palace Theatre straight ahead. The gold statue of ballerina **Anna Pavlova** on top is best viewed from Little Ben, the black clocktower in front of it.

Head right along Victoria Street to Buckingham Gate on the left. Here you can detour by crossing over and then turning left into Christ Church Gardens to view the Suffragette Scroll memorial. Otherwise turn right down Artillery Row. Bear left past the roundabout into Greycoat Place to the Greycoat Hospital school on the right, and the **Greycoat Girl** in one of the alcoves above the entrance.

Continue along Greycoat Place and turn right down Horseferry Road, almost all the way down to Millbank at the end. On the corner of Dean Ryle Street look across at the new office building on the corner of Dean Bradley Street. The statue of **Ada Lovelace** is up at penthouse level.

Cross over Millbank and just before Lambeth Bridge go down the steps on your left into Victoria Tower Gardens, and follow the left-hand edge all the way to the far left corner, where a path takes you to **Emmeline Pankhurst**.

Turn right out of the gardens into Abington Street to Parliament Square. Follow the left-hand edge, and just past St Margaret's Church is the North door of Westminster Abbey. **The Madonna and Child** is between the doors; **Anne of Bohemia** and **Catherine de Valois** with respective spouses are above to the left and right.

Above the West door at the front of the Abbey round the corner are the **Modern Martyrs**.

Cross over Victoria Street to the **Supreme Court**: buxom angels adorn the south balcony facing the Abbey; more sober figures of Mercy and Justice flank the main entrance. Then cross into the centre of Parliament Square: **Millicent Fawcett** faces Big Ben.

Cross Great George Street and head to the corner with Parliament Street. Turn left: you'll pass two **Britannias** on the Department for Sport and Culture building, and another, along with an array of female figures representing **Asia**, **Europe**, etc., on the Foreign Office. Just past the Cenotaph is the **Women of World War II** memorial.

Retrace your steps to Parliament Square and head over Westminster Bridge. **Boudica** is on its left portal. Over the far side on the right the main entrance to St Thomas' Hospital takes you to **Mary Seacole** in the park.

Cross back Westminster Bridge Road and take the Thames Path along the river to the Royal Festival Hall. Turn right along the side of the hall and cross over Belvedere Road to go up Concert Hall Approach and right again along Sutton Walk under the railway bridge. Across the road is Waterloo Station, with **Britannia** above its Victory Arch. **The National Windrush Monument** greets you as you head across the concourse; upstairs at the far end of the mezzanine you'll find *The Sunbathers*.

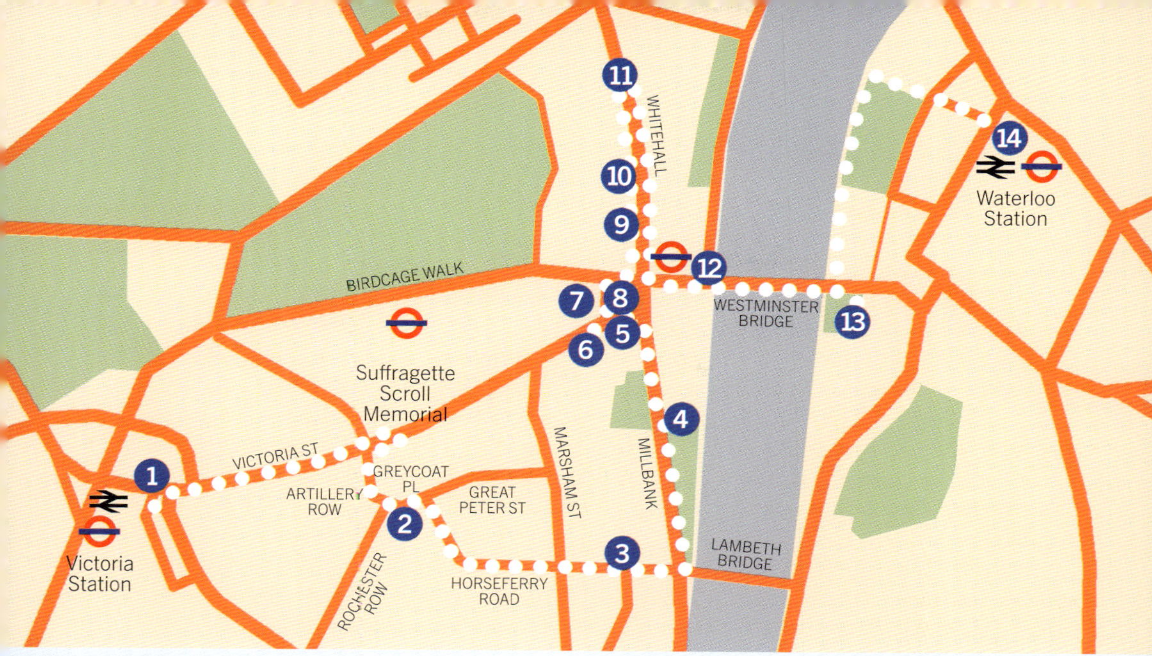

1 Anna Pavlova (p. 28)

2 Greycoat Girl (p. 61)

3 Ada Lovelace (p. 10)

4 Emmeline Pankhurst (p. 64)

5 The Madonna and Child (p. 108)

   Anne of Bohemia and Catherine de Valois (p. 36)

6 Modern Martyrs (p. 132)

7 Supreme Court (p. 178)

8 Millicent Fawcett (p. 134)

9 Two Britannias (p. 42)

10 Asia, Europe (p. 100)

11 Women of World War II (p. 214)

12 Boudica (p. 40)

13 Mary Seacole (p. 126)

14 Britannia (p. 42)

    The National Windrush Monument (p. 208)

    The Sunbathers (p. 103)

Statue Safari 2: Bloomsbury and Covent Garden

We begin with the **Britannia** beside the clocktower on top of St Pancras Station, best viewed from the piazza in front of King's Cross Station on the corner of St Pancras Road.

Turn right along Euston Road, and beyond Euston Station turn left down Gordon Street to Gordon Square, with a gate into the garden on the left. **Noor Inayat Khan** is in the left-hand corner. Exit by the kiosk at the far end and turn left. Enter Tavistock Square opposite the Tavistock Hotel. **Virginia Woolf** is round to the left, **Louisa Brandreth Aldrich-Blake** to the right.

Turn left out of the garden along Tavistock Place, across Judd Street, then right down Wakefield Street to enter St George's Gardens at the end on the left. **Euterpe** is midway through. Exit the way you came to head along Handel Street, and turn left into Hunter Street, which becomes Grenville Street, past Brunswick Square.

At the T-junction turn right, and then left down Queen Anne's Walk into Queen Square, which you enter on the far side. **Queen Charlotte** is at the top end, a **Mother and Child** statue in the centre. Exit the way you came and turn left, then right along pedestrianised Cosmo Place, left into Southampton Row and then right along Great Russell Street all the way to the **British Museum**, where you'll see the 'muses', from Painting to Architecture in the pediment above the entrance.

Cross the street at the zebra crossing to head down Museum Street, which becomes Drury Lane, past Freemasons' Hall, and turn right along pedestrianised Broad Court. *Young Dancer* is at the far end.

Take Floral Street opposite alongside the Royal Opera House all the way down to Garrick Street opposite the Garrick Club. Turn right and cross over the junction to the corner of Cranbourn Street, where you'll find **Agatha Christie**. (The St Martin's Theatre, still hosting *The Mousetrap*, is in nearby West Street.)

Cranbourn Street takes you across Charing Cross Road towards Leicester Square. Up Leicester Court to the right, high on the wall of the Art Deco Vue cinema, you'll find **Wonder Woman**. **Mary Poppins** is in the far right-hand corner of Leicester Square near McDonalds.

Head diagonally across the square to the far corner, where Irving Street leads to Charing Cross Road. Turn right: **Edith Cavell** is on the far side just before the church of St Martin in the Fields.

Turn right along the top of Trafalgar Square for the mostly martial women in the alcoves along the frontage of the **National Gallery**. Follow the west side of the square past the **Fourth Plinth** to the corner and turn right up Cockspur Street. Flanking the entrance to the Brazilian Embassy in Oceanic House on the corner are two caryatids, **East** and **Britannia**.

Head back round the south side of Trafalgar Square to cross the road three times to the Waterstones on the opposite corner. Follow the Strand up to Charing Cross Station, with **Eleanor of Castile** on the large monument in the forecourt.

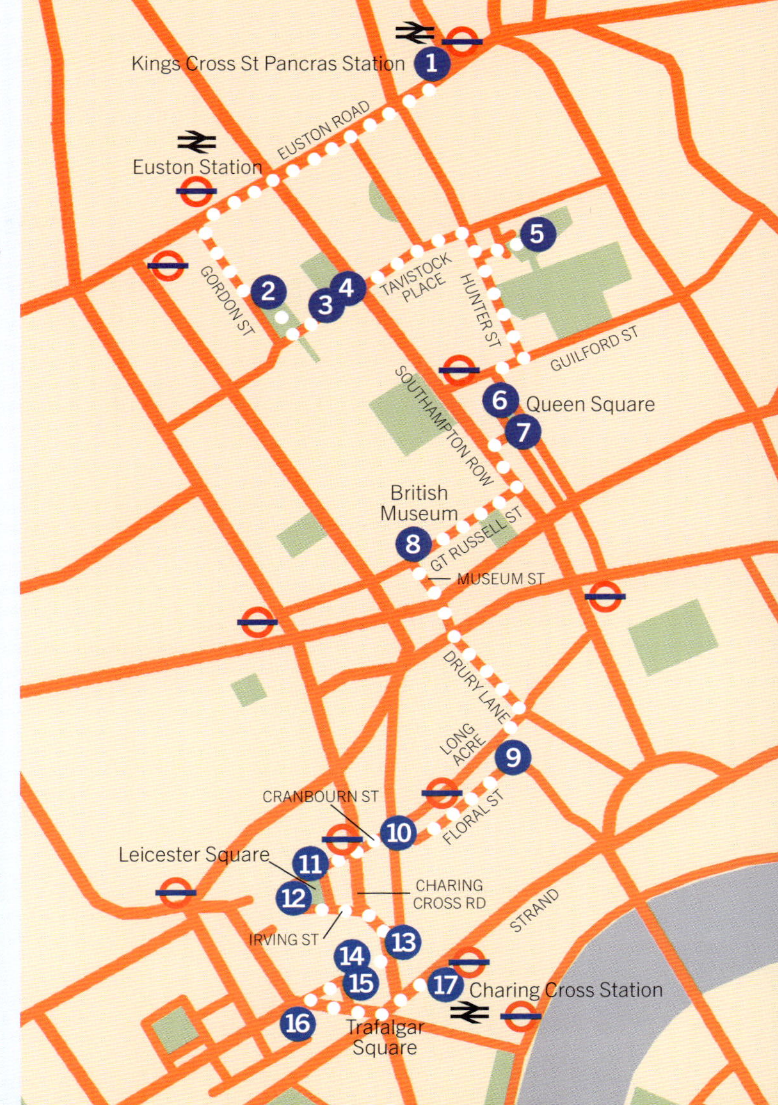

Kings Cross St Pancras Station
1
EUSTON ROAD
Euston Station
5
2
3 4
TAVISTOCK PLACE
GORDON ST
HUNTER ST
GUILFORD ST
6 Queen Square
7
SOUTHAMPTON ROW
British Museum
8
GT RUSSELL ST
MUSEUM ST
DRURY LANE
LONG ACRE
9
CRANBOURN ST
10
FLORAL ST
Leicester Square
11
12
CHARING CROSS RD
IRVING ST
13
STRAND
14
15
17 Charing Cross Station
16
Trafalgar Square

Statue Safari 3: The City

Exit Liverpool Street Station at the eastern end by the escalator by platforms 16/17 and turn left up Bishopsgate. Turn left again up Primrose Street and go up the steps on the left into One Exchange Square. *Rush Hour* is straight ahead, the **Broadgate Venus** beyond.

In the far right-hand corner of the square go down the steps and follow Sun Street Passage (the upper walk) straight ahead until it goes left back into the station. Follow the mezzanine walkway ahead and out to Liverpool Street itself. Turn right along the pedestrianised section to Blomfield Street, and go left and then right into Finsbury Circus. On the far side of the gardens the façade of 1 Finsbury Circus has a **Persian scarf dancer** to the right of the entrance; **Britannia** with a trident is on the corner with Moorgate above the Natwest bank..

Turn left down Moorgate until you cross London Wall. Take Moorgate Place left to the Institute of Chartered Accountants, with **Blind Justice** above the flagstaff on the corner.

Go left along Great Swan Alley, right down Copthall Avenue, bear left then right along pedestrianised Angel Court and left into Throgmorton Street. Pedestrianised Threadneedle Walk takes you to Threadneedle Street: in the square diagonally opposite is **La Maternité drinking fountain**.

Follow Threadneedle Street down to the Bank of England on the corner, with the **Old Lady** above the pediment. Turn right up Princes Street, and detour into the alley on the left to see the bust of **Queen Elizabeth the Queen Mother**

opposite Grocers' Hall. Back on Princes Street you'll see **Ariel** ahead on top of the golden dome and, down Lothbury on the right, the **Ladies of Lothbury** below the pillars.

Across the junction on the left, **13 Moorgate**, on the corner of King's Arms Yard, has six virtues, including Thrift and Self-Denial, on the frontage of this former insurance company headquarters. King's Arms Alley takes you to Coleman Street; turn right and then left through the arcade of Masons Avenue to Basinghall Street. On the Guildhall opposite is the cluster of **Three Queens**; a little further up and round to the left outside the north entrance is *Beyond Tomorrow*.

Follow the side of the Guildhall round into the open space of Guildhall Yard and out onto Gresham Street. Turn right and follow it all the way to cross St Martin's le Grand and take Angel Street opposite to the left. Cross over King Edward Street to Christ Church Greyfriar garden in the nave of a bombed church. **The Christ's Hospital memorial** is on the corner.

Cross the busy junction twice to take pedestrianised Queen's Head Passage opposite, turn right along Paternoster Row to reach Paternoster Square. Temple Bar in the far-left corner has **Anne of Denmark** above the archway; go through to find **Queen Anne** outside the front of St Paul's Cathedral.

Turn left up St Paul's Churchyard, which becomes Cannon Street: just past the cathedral *Two Young Lovers* is in Festival Gardens, the **St Lawrence and St Mary Magdalene drinking fountain** directly across the road. Cannon Street takes you to the mainline station, or Mansion House Tube is nearer.

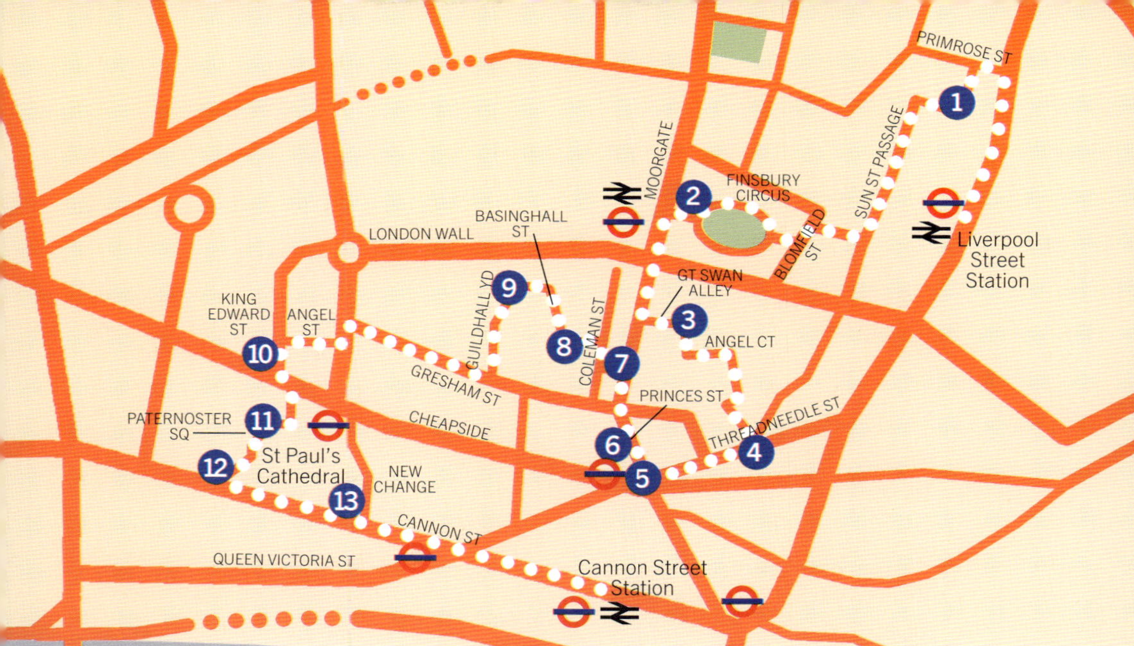

1. *Rush Hour* (p. 76)

The Broadgate Venus (p. 103)

2. Britannia (p. 42)

3. Blind Justice (p. 90)

4. La Maternité drinking fountain (p. 34)

5. Old Lady (p. 80)

Ariel (p. 80)

Ladies of Lothbury (p. 82)

6. Queen Elizabeth the Queen Mother (p. 162)

7. 13 Moorgate (p. 92)

8. Three Queens (p. 159)

9. *Beyond Tomorrow* (p. 101)

10. The Christ's Hospital memorial (p. 60)

11. Anne of Denmark (p. 38)

12. Queen Anne (p. 152)

13. *Two Young Lovers* (p. 100)

St Lawrence and St Mary Magdalene drinking fountain (p. 113)

Chronology: how it all began and where are we now?

1586 Queen Elizabeth I (p. 56X). If this date is correct, then this is the oldest statue not only of an individual woman in London, but also of any named individual.

1630–3 For comparison, the equestrian statue of King Charles I on the south edge of Trafalgar Square is London's oldest public statue of a named man (moved here from Roehampton in 1675 by his son Charles II).

1670–99 If the Queen Elizabeth I was not carved in 1586 then this is its likely date – still the oldest public statue of a named woman in London.

1897 (late May) Lady Henry Somerset Memorial Fountain (p. 94). A statue to a named non-royal woman but not of her – and with other purposes, as it is also a Temperance drinking fountain (p. 32).

1897 (June) Sarah Siddons (p. 176) – the first statue of a named non-royal woman in London. The only one in the nineteenth-century. Sarah Siddons was an actress and popular celebrity.

1902 Boadicea and her Daughters (p. 40). This statue was actually made before Sarah Siddons (the sculptor died in 1885), but not installed until 1902. It would not anyway displace Sarah Siddons, as Boudica (as historians now call her) was royal.

1911 Anna Pavlova (p. 28). Another theatrical celeb.

1914 Margaret MacDonald (p. 106). Often claimed as the first statue of a named non-royal woman as Boudica was royal. The first of several London statues to female social reformers.

1915 Florence Nightingale (p. 66). Also often claimed as the first named non-royal named woman to have a London statue, including in press reports at the time of its unveiling. She was the first of the war women and the first in nursing/medicine. More of both would soon follow.

1920 Edith Cavell (p. 58) – another wartime nurse. Commissioned in 1915, but not unveiled until 1920.

So how does this compare with now?
In the 25 years following the unveiling of London's first statue of a non-royal woman in 1897, only another four were erected (along with quite a few of Queen Victoria, p. 164).

Things have definitely picked up. The first quarter of the twenty-first century has already seen 17 permanent statues to named non-royal women unveiled in the capital, or 24 if you include the Sustrans cut-outs (and why not). That's nearly five times as many as in that initial quarter-century.

Add the royals, and the 25 years of this century have brought us 29 new statues of real women – and counting.

2023 was a bumper year with five new effigies – two queens (Elizabeth II and Victoria), a mathematician (Ada Lovelace), an educator and activist for India (Sister Nivedita) and an 'ordinary' woman (Joy Battick), who was also, back in 1986, the first real woman of colour to have a statue in London (for that chronology see p. 50). Things dropped off again after 2023, but there is reason to hope for a fruitful future.

Index